Library of Shakespearean Biography and Criticism

I. PRIMARY REFERENCE WORKS ON SHAKESPEARE

II. CRITICISM AND INTERPRETATION

    A. Textual Treatises, Commentaries
    B. Treatment of Specal Subjects
    C. Dramatic and Literary Art in Shakespeare

III. SHAKESPEARE AND HIS TIME

    A. General Treatises. Biography
    B. The Age of Shakespeare
    C. Authorship

Series III, Part A

INTRODUCTION

TO

SHAKESPEARE.

PORTRAIT OF SHAKESPEARE.

After Droeshout.

Library of Shakespearean Biography and Criticism

INTRODUCTION

TO

SHAKESPEARE

BY

EDWARD DOWDEN

BOOKS FOR LIBRARIES PRESS

FREEPORT, NEW YORK

First Published 1907
Reprinted 1970

STANDARD BOOK NUMBER:
8369-5254-5

LIBRARY OF CONGRESS CATALOG CARD NUMBER:
78-109645

PRINTED IN THE UNITED STATES OF AMERICA

NOTE.

The publishers of the "Henry Irving Shakespeare" having decided to issue the General Introduction to that edition in a separate
form, I have taken the opportunity to revise what was written, to
add some paragraphs on the great tragedies, and to compile, from
sources easily accessible, a brief notice of the interpretations of
Shakespeare by great actors from Burbage to Macready.

If, in this little volume, there be anything of useful guidance or
suggestion, I desire to connect it with the memory of my wife.

E. D.

CONTENTS.

Page

INTRODUCTION TO SHAKESPEARE:

I. Shakespeare's Life at Stratford and in London, 1

II. The Poetical Creations of his Intellect and
Imagination, - - - - - - 43

III. The Pseudo-Shakespearian Plays, - - 85

IV. Influence of Shakespeare's Works on the
National Mind, - - - - - 88

APPENDIX:

Dedication prefixed to the Folio of 1623, - - 129

Address prefixed to the Folio of 1623, - - - 130

Commendatory Verses from those prefixed to the
Folio of 1623, - - - - - - - 132

Note on the Early Editions of Shakespeare, - 134

Portrait of Shakespeare, after Droeshout, - *frontis.*

Sketch of the Interior of the Swan Theatre, by
Johannes de Witt, - - - - - - 51

INTRODUCTION

TO

SHAKESPEARE.

§1. THE life of Shakespeare has been threefold: first, the external life of good and evil fortune which he lived as a youth in Stratford, as a player and play-wright in London, and again as an honoured inhabitant of his native town; secondly, the inner life of his spirit, the wide-orbing movement of his intellect and imagination of which we can read something in his marvellous series of poetical creations, and can conjecture more; and last, the life which he has lived during three hundred years in the history of the national mind of England, or rather we should say the mind of humanity, the life of posthumous influence which he has exercised, and exercises at the present day, on the generations of mankind. Of each of these it will be our endeavour to speak.

I.

§2. "All that is known with any degree of certainty concerning Shakespeare is—that he was born at Stratford-upon-Avon—married and had children there—went to London, where he commenced actor, and wrote poems and plays—returned to Stratford, made his will, died and was buried." So wrote Steevens a century ago, and De Quincey at a much

more recent date is even briefer in his summing-up
of the facts: "That he lived, and that he died, and
that he was 'a little lower than the angels'—these
make up pretty nearly the amount of our undis-
puted report". Having spoken of the perplexity
which we are likely to feel on finding the materials
for the biography of a transcendent writer so meagre
and so few, De Quincey goes on to solve the
difficulty by an elaborate argument intended to
prove that the parliamentary war and the local
feuds engendered by it extinguished those traditions and memorials of Shakespeare which, he says,
must have been abundant up to that era. In truth
there is no great cause for wonder or perplexity.
More is known of Shakespeare's life than Steevens
and De Quincey allege. More is known of Shakespeare's life than of the lives of many of his dramatic
contemporaries. Far less has been ascertained
respecting the life of Marlowe, whose fame stood
so high in Elizabethan days, and whose personality
was undoubtedly a striking one. Far less has been
ascertained respecting the life of Webster or the life
of Ford, although these dramatists flourished at a
later time, and one of them was a gentleman of position. The materials for John Fletcher's biography
are of the scantiest kind; it is not certain whether
he went to Cambridge; it is not certain whether
he lived and died unmarried; from 1593 to 1607
his history is a complete blank. Yet Fletcher was
highly honoured by his contemporaries; he survived
till the opening of the reign of Charles I.; his father
was the Bishop of London. The Elizabethan age
was not an age of literary biography; a playwright,

unless, like Ben Jonson, he were distinguished for his scholarship and classical learning, was hardly thought of as a man of letters. Our wonder as regards Shakespeare should be, not that we know so little, but that we know so much. Our acquaintance with the facts of his outward history—partly founded on tradition, partly on documents—is due to the zeal of lovers of the great dramatist, from the actor Betterton to the latest and most indefatigable of investigators, Mr. Halliwell-Phillipps. We cannot hope that much additional light will ever be gained. The facts which we possess are enough to assure us that the greatest of poets conducted his material life, after, perhaps, some errors of his ardent youth, wisely and well to a prosperous issue. They are enough to prove his good sense and discreet dealing in worldly affairs.

§ 3. Richard Shakespeare, the poet's grandfather, was a Warwickshire farmer, renting land at Snitterfield, a village some three or four miles from Stratford-on-Avon. His son John, evidently a man of some enterprise and energy, settled at Stratford about 1551, and did business in Henley Street as a fellmonger and glover. According to Aubrey he was a butcher, and it may be that he slaughtered the beasts whose skins he converted into gauntlets and leggings; according to Rowe he was a considerable dealer in wool, and it is certain that he had transactions in corn and in timber. In 1557 he greatly improved his position by his marriage with Mary, the youngest and the favourite daughter of Robert Arden, a wealthy farmer, lately deceased, of the neighbouring hamlet of Wilmecote. That

these Ardens were connected with an ancient family
of gentlefolk of that name has been asserted, and
may be true, but the statement cannot be proved.
Mary Arden inherited from her father an estate of
some sixty acres, known as Asbies, at Wilmecote,
together with the reversion to part of a larger property at Snitterfield, on which Snitterfield property
her father-in-law, Richard Shakespeare, held land
as a tenant. From this date John Shakespeare
became a person of some importance at Stratford,
and he rose year by year in the esteem of his fellow-
townsmen. Appointed at first by the corporation
one of the officers whose duty it was to supervise
malt liquors and bread, he became in 1561 a
chamberlain of the borough, in 1565 an alderman,
and in 1568 he was elected to the most important
official position in the town, that of high bailiff.
It is true that he could not write even his name,
but the accomplishment of penmanship was rare
among the members of the corporation. He was
certainly a successful man of business and a skilful
accountant.

§4. In the house in Henley Street towards the close
of April, 1564, was born William Shakespeare, the
eldest son of his parents. Two daughters, who died
in infancy, had been born before him. On April
the 26th the child was baptized; a tradition of the
last century, that Shakespeare died upon his birthday, would favour the popular opinion that he was
born on April 23rd; but his monument states that
he died in his fifty-third year. Attention was called
by De Quincey to the fact that Shakespeare's only
grandchild, Elizabeth Hall, was married to Thomas

Nash on April 22nd, and he suggested that the day may have been chosen as the anniversary of her grandfather's birthday. The matter remains doubtful. April the 23rd, Old Style, corresponds with our present May 5th.

Stratford-on-Avon, in which Shakespeare spent his youth and to which he gladly returned in his elder years, was a town of gable-roofed, timber or timber-and-plaster houses, containing some fourteen or fifteen hundred inhabitants. Its chief buildings were the noble church hard by the river, and the Guildhall where on occasions travelling companies of actors would present their plays. Around it in Warwickshire, "the heart of England", lay the perfection of rural landscape: in the Feldon division such pasture-lands, with a wealth of wild flowers, as Shakespeare has described in A Winter's Tale; and in the Arden division the perfection of forest scenery, such woodland glades and streams as he has imagined in the French Arden of As You Like It. During the Wars of the Roses the county was divided against itself; Coventry was Lancastrian, Warwick, for a time, Yorkist. The battle of Bosworth Field was fought near its north-eastern border. Traditions of the stirring events of those times must have lived on to Shakespeare's day, and created in his imagination a sympathy with the great historical figures of that period which he has represented with such life and force in his historical dramas.

That Shakespeare was sent to the Free School at Stratford is stated by his first biographer, Rowe, and we may reasonably assume that such was the

fact. Some knowledge of reading and writing was
required at entrance; the usual age of pupils when
admitted was seven. When duly drilled in the
Latin accidence (of which we have an amusing
Shakespearian reminiscence in Sir Hugh Evans'
examination of William Page in The Merry Wives
of Windsor), the boy began to construe from the
Sententiæ Pueriles, and, if he remained long enough
at school, advanced as far as Ovid, Virgil, Cicero,
and the Eclogues of Mantuanus. Much has been
written on the subject of Shakespeare's learning.
From Ben Jonson's scholarly point of view he may
be said to have had "small Latin and less Greek".
Perhaps the Greek was nothing or next to nothing;
but Aubrey was probably not wrong when he stated
on the authority of a Mr. Beeston that Shakespeare
"understode Latine pretty well". In later years he
seems to have acquired a little knowledge of French,
and possibly a little knowledge of Italian.

§ 5. At what age Shakespeare was withdrawn from
school we cannot tell. But we know that when he
was thirteen years old his father was no longer a
prosperous man, and that the fortunes of his house
continued for a considerable time to decline. While
John Shakespeare's means were first waxing and
then rapidly waning, his family had increased in
numbers. His son Gilbert, who afterwards became
a haberdasher in London and who lived certainly
to 1609, was born in 1566; Joan, who was married
to William Hart, and whose name appears in the
great dramatist's will, was born 1569; Anne, born
in 1571, died in her eighth year; Richard, born in
March 1573-74, lived to manhood, dying at Stratford

in 1613; John Shakespeare's last child, Edmund,
born in 1580, became an actor, died in September
1607, and on the morning of his burial at St.
Saviour's, Southwark, a knell of the "great bell"
of the church was rung, a mark of respect secured
only by the payment of a considerable fee. Thus
with younger brothers and a sister requiring susten-
ance and education, and with narrowing means in
the household, William Shakespeare, at the age of
thirteen may, as the tradition asserts, have been set
to help his father in business. An old parish clerk
of Stratford towards the close of the seventeenth
century declared that Shakespeare was bound
apprentice to a butcher; and according to Aubery
he performed the sacrificial rites with dramatic
accompaniments, for "when he killed a calf, he
would do it in a high style and make a speech".
According to another report he was a country
schoolmaster, and Malone has argued from Shakespeare's frequent and exact use of law-terms that
most probably he was for two or three years in the
office of a Stratford attorney. We may indulge
our imagination by picturing the future poet rather
as a wool-stapler than as a butcher's lad.

What cannot be doubted is that his father had
passed from wealth to comparative poverty. In
1578 he effected a large mortgage on the estate of
Asbies; when he tendered payment in the following
year it was refused until other sums due had been
repaid; the money designed for the redemption of
Asbies had been obtained by the sale of his wife's
reversionary interest in the Snitterfield property.
His taxes were lightened, nor was he always able

to pay those which were still claimed. He dropped off from attendance at the town-council, and in consequence was ultimately deprived of his alderman's gown (1586). He fell into debt, and was tormented with legal proceedings. A commission appointed to inquire respecting Jesuits, priests, and recusants reported his name in 1592 among those of persons who "come not to church for fear of process for debt". It does not appear, however, that he was obliged to part with his house in Henley Street, and, as we shall see, his eldest son was careful, when prosperity came to him in his dramatic career, to restore the fallen fortunes of his father.

§ 6. Before he was nineteen years old Shakespeare had a new and a powerful motive for trying to better himself in the world; he had taken to himself a wife. A bond given before the marriage, for the security of the bishop in licensing the marriage after once asking of the banns, is preserved in the registry at Worcester. It is dated November 28, 1582. The bride, Anne Hathaway, the daughter of a substantial yeoman, lately deceased, of Shottery hamlet in the parish of Stratford, was between seven and eight years older than her husband. The sureties of the bond were friends of the Hathaway family, and the seal of Anne's father was used on the occasion, whence it has been inferred that the Shottery folk rather than those of Henley Street were desirous of the match. Whether the consent of Shakespeare's parents was or was not given we have no means of ascertaining. Shakespeare's eldest child—Susanna—was baptized on May 26, 1583, just six months after the bond, preliminary to

marriage, had been signed. The ceremony of wedlock may have been preceded by precontract, which
according to the custom of the time and place would
have been looked on as having the validity of
marriage, though as yet unsanctified by ecclesiastical
rites. Halliwell-Phillipps has aptly pointed out
that when Shakespeare's maternal grandfather,
Robert Arden, "settled part of an estate on his
daughter Agnes, on July the seventeenth, 1550, he
introduces her as *nunc uxor Thome Stringer, ac
nuper uxor Johannis Hewyns*, and yet the marriage
was not solemnized until three months afterwards".
It may be added that the words "wedded wife"
were at this time in no way tautological; a woman
duly espoused might be a wife though the priestly
benediction of wedlock had not yet been bestowed.

The marriage of a boy of eighteen with a woman
eight years his senior, of humbler rank than his own
and probably uneducated, cannot be called prudent;
but we have no evidence to prove that the union
was unhappy. Shakespeare remained in Stratford
with his wife until he went to seek his fortune in
London. Although he did not bring her and her
children to the capital, he certainly from time to
time visited his home. He looked forward to
returning to his native town, and living henceforth
by her side, and he actually carried that long-con-
templated purpose into effect. It may be, as
Shakespeare's Sonnets seem to indicate, that for a
season his heart was led astray by the intellectual
fascination of a woman who possessed all those
qualities of brilliance and cultured grace which
perhaps were lacking in his wife; but if so, Shake-

B

speare perceived his error, and in due time returned
to the companion of his youth.   In his will he
leaves her only his "second best bed with the
furniture", and this as an afterthought, for the
words occur as an interlineation; but without
special bequest she was sufficiently provided for
by free-bench and dower; the best bed, as Mr.
Halliwell-Phillipps suggests, was probably that re-
served for strangers, the second best may have been
that of the master and mistress of the house.   We
cannot suppose that the wife of his early choice,
the daughter of a husbandman, could have followed
Shakespeare in his poetical mountings of mind or
in his profound dramatic studies of character, but
there is a wide field for mutual sympathy and help
in the common joys and sorrows and daily tasks
of household life, and the greatest of men are
sometimes they who can best value the qualities of
homely goodness.   We cannot think of Shakespeare's marriage as a rare union of perfect accord,
but we are not justified in speaking of it as unfortunate.   In A Midsummer Night's Dream Lysander
has a reference to love "misgraffed in respect of
years"; in Twelfth Night the Duke warns Viola,
when disguised in the garb of a youth, against the
danger of an unequal marriage:—

> Let still the woman take
> An elder than herself; so wears she to him,
> So sways she level in her husband's heart.—(ii. 4. 30–32.)

Even if the lines were non-dramatic, they would
prove no more than that the writer with good sense
admitted as a rule that to which his own experience

may have been the exception.   One other passage
from the plays has been cited as bearing on Shake-
peare's marriage, that passage in The Tempest where
Prospero, after he has given his daughter to Ferdinand as his future bride, cautions the Prince against
"breaking her virgin-knot" before

> All sanctimonious ceremonies may
> With full and holy rite be minister'd.—(IV. I. 16, 17.)

The Tempest was probably written to grace some
noble wedding, and Shakespeare's mature wisdom
of life, uttering itself through Prospero, recognized
the fact that the sanctity of marriage can hardly be
guarded with too great jealousy.   Having closed
the series of his dramatic works, perhaps with the
very play in which this passage occurs, he returned
to his home to find the happiness of his elder years
in company with her whom he had loved in boyhood.

§ 7. For three or four years after his marriage Shakespeare continued to reside at Stratford, and in 1585
his wife gave birth to twins, a boy and girl, baptized
(Feb. 2) Hamnet and Judith, doubtless after Hamnet
Sadler, a baker of Stratford, and Judith his wife.
For this Hamnet Sadler, presumably sponsor for
the boy, who, to the grief of his father, died before
he had reached the age of twelve (buried August 11,
1596), Shakespeare retained a regard to the close
of his life.   He is remembered in the great dramatist's will, where the name appears in the form
"Hamlett" Sadler, receiving a bequest of one pound
six and eightpence "to buy him a ringe".

In what employments and with what recreations
these years at Stratford, growing years of early man-

hood, went by we can but conjecture. How they came to a close we are told by Shakespeare's first biographer, Rowe: "He had by a misfortune, common enough to young fellows, fallen into ill company, and amongst them, some that made a frequent practice of deer-stealing, engaged him more than once in robbing a park that belonged to Sir Thomas Lucy, of Charlcote, near Stratford. For this he was prosecuted by that gentleman, as he thought, somewhat too severely; and in order to revenge that ill usage, he made a ballad upon him. And though this, probably the first essay of his poetry, be lost, yet it is said to have been so very bitter, that it redoubled the prosecution against him to that degree, that he was obliged to leave his business and family in Warwickshire, for some time, and shelter himself in London." According to Archdeacon Davies, vicar of Sapperton in the county of Gloucester, who died in 1708, Sir Thomas Lucy had the young poacher "oft whipped and sometimes imprisoned", in revenge for which Shakespeare afterwards made him "his Justice Clodpate [Justice Shallow: *clodpate* meaning foolish] and calls him a great man, and that in allusion to his name bore three louses rampant for his arms". The first stanza of the ballad which Rowe speaks of as lost is given by Oldys on the authority of "a very aged gentleman living in the neighbourhood of Stratford", and it contains the same offensive play on the name Lucy—"O lowsie Lucy"—as that in the passage to which Davies refers.

We can hardly doubt that there is a kernel of truth in these traditions. Malone endeavoured to

disprove the deer-stealing story by showing that
Sir Thomas Lucy had no park at Charlcote; but
he may have had deer there; or the scene of the
adventure, instead of Charlcote, may have been the
adjoining sequestered estate of Fulbroke, over which
Sir Thomas, as a local magnate devoted to the
crown, may have kept watch and ward. It has been
suggested that he may have felt some animosity
against the Shakespeare family as possibly having
sympathy with the old religion, for Sir Thomas was
not only a game preserver but a zealous Protestant.
The offence of poaching was commonly regarded at
the time by those who did not suffer from it as a
venial frolic of youth; "the students of Oxford, the
centre of the kingdom's learning and intelligence,"
says Halliwell-Phillipps, "had been for many generations the most notorious poachers in all England".
There can be no doubt that Shakespeare retained
some ill-will against the Lucy family. In The Merry
Wives of Windsor Justice Shallow fumes with violent indignation against Sir John Falstaff, whom he
charges with having beaten his men, killed his deer,
and broken open his lodge. We are informed by Slender that in the Shallow coat of arms are a "dozen
white luces", translated by Evans, the Welsh parson,
with unconscious humour, into "a dozen white louses"
which "do become an old coat well". Sir Thomas
was a member of that strong Protestant commission
which reported that Shakespeare's father did not
attend church in 1592 for fear of process for debt,
a circumstance which might have kept the early
soreness of feeling from subsiding. If it is any
satisfaction to us we have some reason to believe

that the barb prepared for Sir Thomas Lucy struck home, and that the family did not forget the mockery of their old coat. A copy of the 1619 Quarto edition of The Merry Wives of Windsor was discovered not very long since among the family records, the only copy of any one of Shakespeare's plays in the early editions found at Charlcote.

§ 8. In what year Shakespeare quitted Stratford we cannot tell; it can hardly have been earlier than 1585, and may have been a year or two later. Nor can we say with certainty how he came to join himself to a company of players. From early childhood he had opportunities of seeing dramatic perform- ances. Perhaps he inherited from his father a taste for the drama; theatrical entertainments, as has been noticed by Halliwell-Phillipps, are first heard of at Stratford-on-Avon during the year of John Shake- speare's bailiffship. While the players declaimed in the Guildhall the boy may have looked on, standing between his father's legs, as his contemporary Willis tells us he did when he saw The Cradle of Security acted before the aldermen and common council of the city of Gloucester. He may have witnessed the performance of the mysteries at Coventry on the Corpus Christi festival; his phrase " out-herods Herod" is a reminiscence of the ramping and raging king by whose command the innocents of Bethlehem were slaughtered; his comparison of the flea on Bardolph's fiery nose to "a black soul burning in hell-fire" was the grotesque fancy of one who had probably watched the exhibition of the damned with their sooty faces and black and yellow garb in the pageant at Coventry. Various companies of

players visited Stratford from time to time and performed under the patronage of the corporation;
before Shakespeare forsook his home, says Dyce,
" he had doubtless seen the best dramatic produc-
tions, such as they were, represented by the best
actors then alive". He may have made acquaintance with some of the London players, but the
assertion that the famous Burbage was from Warwickshire, and that Thomas Greene, an actor of
James I.'s time, was a Stratford man, have been
made without sufficient evidence. Leicester's players
visited Stratford in 1587; it is supposed by Mr.
Fleay that Shakespeare joined them during or immediately after their arrival, and during their travels
received his earliest instruction in comic acting from
Kempe and Pope, who soon after became noted
performers.[1]   But this is mere conjecture, and the
early traditions do not favour the notion that Shakespeare left his native town with the design of taking
to the stage.   They rather lead us to believe that
after his arrival in London he gradually found his
way towards his future profession.

According to a tradition, which is alleged to have
come down to us through Sir William D'Avenant,
the first employment of Shakespeare in connection
with the theatre was that of holding the horses of
gentlemen who had ridden to the playhouse. The
first building erected (1576) for the exhibition of
dramatic performances in England was that known
as " The Theatre", situated in the parish of Shoreditch.   It was the property of James Burbage, father

[1] A Chronicle History of the Life and Work of William Shakespeare,
by F. G. Fleay, p. 8.

of Shakespeare's fellow-actor, the great tragedian, Richard Burbage. James Burbage kept livery-stables close by Smithfield, and it is an ingenious suggestion of Halliwell-Phillipps that, on arriving in London, Shakespeare may have sold at Smithfield the horse on which he rode up to town, may then and there have made the acquaintance of James Burbage, and may have been employed by him to take care of the horses of Burbage's Smithfield customers who visited the theatre. The tradition adds that Shakespeare made himself popular, and soon had to hire lads to assist him, who, "when Will Shakespeare was summoned were immediately to present themselves, ' I am Shakespeare's boy, sir'"; whence the young lackeys, after their master's fortune had raised him to higher employment, continued to be known as "Shakespeare's Boys". An old parish-clerk of Stratford, towards the close of the seventeenth century, informed visitors that the dramatist was first received into the playhouse as " a serviture", that is, as an attendant on the players. The stage-tradition of a hundred years ago was that he acted as the prompter's assistant, giving the performers notice to be ready when their presence was required on the stage.

§ 9. It is not surprising that Shakespeare's early years in connection with the theatre should have left no record behind them. We know that he did not cut himself adrift from Stratford and his own family, for in 1587 he joined his father in an effort to assign the title of the Asbies property to John Lambert in consideration of the cancelling of the previous mortgage and the payment of £20. But

beyond this fact we know nothing for certain until
1592, when he was an author and an actor, and of
importance in both capacities to his dramatic company. A year before this, in 1591, was published
Spenser's poem, The Tears of the Muses, in which
Thalia, the Muse of Comedy, laments the cessation
from authorship of some creator of general mirth
whom Spenser names "our pleasant Willy":

> And he, the man whom Nature selfe had made
>   To mock her selfe, and Truth to imitate,
> With kindly counter under mimic shade,
>   Our pleasant Willy, ah! is dead of late.

It would be pleasant to suppose that the author of
the Faerie Queene here spoke of his great contemporary; but it is much more probable that Spenser's
friend, the dramatist John Lyly, is meant.[1] If
Spenser ever refers to Shakespeare, it is in his Colin
Clouts Come Home Again, in lines which describe
some high poet under the name of "Aetion", the
eaglet (from ἀετός, an eagle). Colin Couts was not
published until 1594, but probably was written in
whole or in part in 1591. The true name of
"Aetion" had, says Spenser, a heroic sound, which
agrees well with the name Shakespeare; the epithet
"gentle" seems to be one to which our poet had
almost a peculiar right:

> And there, though last not least, is Aetion,
>   A gentler shepheard may no where be found:
> Whose Muse, full of high thoughts invention,
>   Doth like himselfe heroically sound.

---

[1] Halliwell-Phillipps identifies "our pleasant Willy" with the comic
actor Richard Tarlton (died 1588); Professor Minto supposes him to be
Sir Philip Sidney.

These lines, if written as early as 1591, were hardly
meant for Shakespeare; they may, however, be a
later insertion.   But it seems not unlikely that
Drayton was intended, who had written under the
poetical name of " Rowland", and whose Idea, as
some have thought, may be pointed to (though to
myself the notion appears far-fetched) by the choice
of the name Aetion ($ἰδέα = αἴτιον$).

§ 10. There can be no mistake that Shakespeare
is the object of Greene's attack in the pamphlet
Greenes Groatsworth of Wit bought with a Million
of Repentance, written by the unhappy poet as he
lay dying in a mean house in Dowgate, attended
by a shoemaker's wife, his kind hostess and nurse.
The pamphlet must have been written in August,
1592.   Having warned his friends Marlowe, Peele,
and "young Juvenal" (probably Lodge) against the
inconstancy of the players, he proceeds: "Yes, trust
them not: for there is an upstart Crow, beautified
with our feathers, that with his *Tygers heart wrapt
in a Players hide*, supposes he is as well able to
bumbast out a blanke verse as the best of you: and
being an absolute *Iohannes fac totum*, is in his owne
conceit the onely Shake-scene in a countrie ".   The
travestied line

> Oh tiger's heart wrapt in a woman's hide,

is found in Richard, Duke of York, and also in the
Third Part of Henry VI., which is founded on Richard,
Duke of York.   In the old play Marlowe and Greene
had probably been collaborateurs, and it would seem
that Greene bitterly resented Shakespeare's rehandling of his work, and felt indignant at the success

of one whom he looked on as an unlettered rival. Greene's pamphlet was seen through the press by Henry Chettle, and in December of the same year he entered on the Stationers' Books his own prose tract Kind-Hart's Dreame, in the preface to which he apologizes to Shakespeare for Greene's unworthy attack. He expresses his regret for not having used his discretion in moderating the writer's warmth; he is as sorry, he says, as if the original fault were his own, "because my selfe have seene his [Shakespeare's] demeanour no less civil than he exelent in the qualitie he professes: Besides, divers of worship have reported his uprightness of dealing, which argues his honesty, and his facetious [i.e. felicitous] grace in writing, that approves his Art". The word "quality" in this passage of Chettle's "Address to the Gentlemen Readers" of his pamphlet has a special reference to the profession of an actor, as it has in Hamlet's inquiry respecting the boy-performers: "Will they pursue the quality no longer than they can sing?" We may infer from Chettle's words that Shakespeare was at least a respectable actor. According to Rowé, "the top of his performance was the Ghost in his own *Hamlet*," a part requiring an actor of good delivery though not a great artist. There is some ground for thinking that he played the part of Old Knowell in Jonson's Every Man in His Humour, in the representation of which comedy he certainly appeared. And there is a confused tradition handed down by Oldys which makes it probable that he was the Adam of his own As You Like It. Whether he excelled or not in his practice as an actor, Shakespeare certainly had a cultivated knowledge of the principles of the histrionic art; the instructions given to the players by Hamlet could have come from no one who had not carefully studied the merits and the defects of the actor on the boards; the writer of the words assigned to Hamlet assuredly knew the grace of moderation and reserve in the rendering of passion, and at the same time knew the error of languor or inertness. The latest express mention of Shakespeare as having taken a part in the performance of a play is in connection with Ben Jonson's Sejanus, which was performed at the Globe Theatre in 1603 or 1604. But in a document of 1610 the Burbages speak of placing Shakespeare as an actor among others at Blackfriars Theatre. His name, however, does not appear in a list of the actors of The Alchemist (1610), in which, if he were then performing, he might naturally have taken a part among his fellows.

§ 11. No doubt it was perceived at an early date in Shakespeare's dramatic company that he could aid them more by his pen than by his voice. As we learn from the charges and insinuations of Greene, part of Shakespeare's early work as a writer for the stage was that of revising and adapting the work of his predecessors or early contemporaries. It was an excellent way of apprenticeship to his dramatic craft. He learned to distinguish between what is effective and ineffective on the stage; he acquired the art of carrying on the action of a piece without falling into tedious speech-making, he studied the links and transitions of the dramatic events, he came to see how these should be manipulated, he learned how to develop a dramatic char-

acter, how to regulate imagery and diction so that
they should never pass into the epical; and while
amending the pieces of others his own genius would
have enough of play to gain in strength, and enough
of restraint to save it from the waste of exuberant
power.

But the poet in Shakespeare could not be content
with what may be justly described as in a certain
degree hackwork. The poet in Shakespeare aspired
to an independent existence, and apparently he did
not yet perceive that through the drama alone could
his genius explore the heights and depths of passion
and of song. In the passage quoted from Kind-
Hart's Dreame the author informs his readers that
"divers of worship" have reported to him Shakespeare's "facetious grace in writing". Possibly
Shakespeare had already earned the good opinion
and good-will of the Earl of Southampton. Early
in 1593 Richard Field, the son of a Stratford
tanner, himself a London printer, was carrying
through the press Shakespeare's Venus and Adonis,
which was published in that year with a dedication
to Southampton, in which the author, speaking of
his young patron with graceful homage and of his
poem with becoming modesty, describes it as "the
first heire of my invention". Doubtless several plays
of merit by Shakespeare had already appeared upon
the stage; but they had not been published by the
press; they formed in the eyes of Shakespeare's
contemporaries hardly a part of literature proper;
they could not compete in dignity with such a
miniature epic as this which now appeared, and in
which Shakespeare first claimed his rank as poet.

Venus and Adonis at once became popular, and edition followed edition during a series of years. In the dedication Shakespeare promises that if his poem should please the earl, he would take advantage of all idle hours to prepare some "graver labour" for his patron's honour. This graver labour, the Lucrece, followed in 1594; graver because of its tragic theme, and its celebration of the wronged, yet triumphant, purity of woman. It is dedicated to Southampton in words of loyal affection: "What I have done is yours, what I have to do is yours, being part in all I have, devoted yours"; and a reference to favours received proves that the regard and esteem were not on Shakespeare's side alone. "There is", says Rowe, "one instance so singular in the magnificence of this patron of Shakespeare's, that, if I had not been assured that the story was handed down by Sir William D'Avenant, who was probably very well acquainted with his affairs, I should not have ventured to have inserted; that my Lord Southampton at one time gave him a thousand pounds to enable him to go through with a purchase which he heard he had a mind to". It is supposed that the purchase was that of the large house named New Place in the centre of the town of Stratford-on-Avon, which Shakespeare bought for £60 in the spring of 1597, a gabled house of brick, resting on stone foundations, with a bay-window on the garden side. Report—if this be so— exaggerated the amount of Southampton's gift, but even sixty pounds in the days of Elizabeth was a very considerable sum of money.

§ 12. In December, 1594, Shakespeare appeared in

two comedies before Queen Elizabeth at Greenwich Palace. Two eminent actors of his company, that known as the Lord Chamberlain's servants, Richard Burbage, the tragedian, and Kemp, a popular comedian, were associated with him on this occasion.[1] The queen, who had a keen eye for merit, honoured Shakespeare and his art. Ben Jonson in his memorial lines prefixed to the First Folio speaks of those "flights" of the "Swan of Avon"

> upon the bankes of Thames,
> That so did take Eliza, and our Iames.

Shakespeare's company repeatedly performed before the queen at Richmond Palace, at Greenwich Palace, at Whitehall. In the Christmas holidays of 1597 her Majesty witnessed a performance of Love's Labour's Lost in its revised form, "newly corrected and augmented". Next Christmas three plays were given at Whitehall, among them probably The Merry Wives of Windsor, by Elizabeth's express desire. It is a well-known tradition that the queen was so highly entertained by Falstaff, as seen in the two parts of King Henry IV., that she commanded the dramatist to continue the character for one play more, and show the fat knight in love. That bright comedy of English rural life, The Merry Wives, is said to have been the work of a fortnight. At times, by special arrangement, Shake-

---

[1] Halliwell-Phillipps's statement as to the companies to which Shakespeare belonged previously to his joining the Lord Chamberlain's servants deserves to be quoted: " It would appear not altogether unlikely that the poet was one of Lord Strange's actors in March, 1592; one of Lord Pembroke's a few months later; and that he joined the company of the Earl of Sussex in or before January, 1594 ". But on this subject see especially Mr. Fleay's A Chronicle History of the Life and Work of William Shakespeare.

speare's plays were performed for the grave lawyers
of the Inns of Court in their mirth-loving hours of
leisure. On Innocents' Day, 1594, the day after
Shakespeare's performance before the queen at
Greenwich, The Comedy of Errors was presented
before a distinguished company in the hall of Gray's
Inn; there had been some confusion and disturbance
in the earlier part of the evening, which ceased while
the spectators watched the entanglements of the
twins of Syracuse and Ephesus; ever afterwards
that night of Dec. 28, 1594, was remembered as the
Night of Errors. Early in February, 1601–2, the
benchers of the Middle Temple witnessed in their
hall (which still exists) a performance of that delightful comedy Twelfth Night; the law student
John Manningham records the fact in his diary,
and tells us of his diversion at the odd figure of the
deluded Malvolio. But of these occasional performances by Shakespeare's company the most remarkable were two which took place in the preceding year. On February 8th, 1601, the Earl of
Essex, accompanied by Shakespeare's patron, Henry
Wriothesley, Earl of Southampton, and Roger Manners, Earl of Rutland, made their rash revolt in the
streets of London. On the preceding afternoon, by
special arrangement between the conspirators and
the Lord Chamberlain's servants, "a play of the
deposing and killing of King Richard" [i.e. possibly
Shakespeare's King Richard II.] was represented
at the Globe Theatre.[1] It was not a new play, and

[1] Shakespeare's play was already in print, but the earlier quartos—
those published in Elizabeth's reign—do not contain the deposition
scene, lines 154–318 of act iv. sc. 1.

the actors, to provide against loss if the attendance
should be small, required that the sum of forty shillings should be added by their employers to whatever might be taken at the door.   Less than two
years previously, in this same Globe Theatre, Shakespeare's lines in honour of Essex, then her Majesty's
representative in Ireland, had been delivered as part
of the prologue to the last act of King Henry V.
The unfortunate earl was executed on February 25.
Perhaps to make an outward show of equanimity,
Elizabeth spent the evening before his execution in
witnessing at Richmond Palace a dramatic performance by the same company of actors who, a few
days previously, had been employed to prepare the
minds of the Londoners for the treasonable outbreak of the doomed favourite.   When the queen
died, in 1603, it was noticed in print by Henry
Chettle, the former editor of Greene's pamphlet, that
Shakespeare did not join in the poetical lamentations of the time.

§ 13. James I. had not been many days in London before he granted a license to the members of
Shakespeare's company to enact plays both in town
and in the provinces.   In December, 1603, while
the king was a visitor at Wilton, the seat of William
Herbert, Earl of Pembroke, they received a call to
perform before the royal party.   The editors of the
First Folio of Shakespeare's plays (1623), in the
dedication of that volume, addressing William Herbert and his brother Philip, Earl of Montgomery,
refer to the great favour which these patrons of art
had shown both to the author of the plays and the
plays themselves.   When his Majesty's long-delayed

state entry into London took place, Shakespeare
and his fellows appeared in the king's train: "each
of them was presented with four yards and a half
of scarlet cloth, the usual dress allowance to players
belonging to the household. The poet and his col-
leagues were termed the king's servants, and took
rank at court amongst the Grooms of the Chamber."[1] We have records (copied for Malone) of the
performance by the king's servants at Whitehall of
Othello (Nov. 1, 1604), of Measure for Measure
(Dec. 26, 1604), and of King Lear (Dec. 26, 1606).
The lines in Measure for Measure (ii. 4. 24–30)
which describe the troubles of a king occasioned
by the over-demonstrative loyalty of his admiring
subjects, and those in Macbeth which tell of the
cure of the king's-evil by the royal touch, are supposed to have been meant as compliments to King
James.

During the summer and early autumn months
the players often itinerated. Thus in the summer
of 1597 Shakespeare's company travelled through
Sussex and Kent; on Sept. 3rd they acted at
Dover, where, as Halliwell-Phillipps has observed,
the author of Lear might have seen the samphire
gatherers on the cliff, which may have served as
model for Edgar's imaginary precipice. They turned
westward in that year, reached Bristol, and performed at Marlborough and Bath. In the autumn
of 1605 they travelled to Barnstaple, and before
returning to town acted before the mayor and corporation of Oxford. In that city of spires and

---

[1] Halliwell-Phillipps: Outlines of the Life of Shakespeare, vol. i.
p. 212.

colleges Shakespeare probably lodged at John
D'Avenant's tavern, and knew the tavern-keeper's
handsome wife. Her boy, the future dramatist, Sir
William D'Avenant, born in March, 1606, was re-
puted to be Shakespeare's godson. The gossip
which named our poet as father of the boy has no
real evidence to lend it support.

§ 14. The playhouse in which Shakespeare first
acted, if not "The Theatre" which belonged to
James Burbage, must have been that named "The
Curtain", which stood not far off in a division of
the parish of Shoreditch known as the Liberty of
Halliwell (holy well). Here, on the edge of the
great city, the country had actually begun; we read
of a prentice in the year 1584 sleeping on the grass
"very nere the Theatre or Curten". In 1598 The
Theatre had ceased to be suitable for the require-
ments of the time, and in the winter of that year
(Dec.-Jan. 1598–99) the timber of which it was
built was removed to Southwark with a view to its
forming part of a new and better structure. This
building, known as The Globe, from its sign of
Hercules or Atlas carrying his load, stood not far
from London Bridge, a little westward, and close
to the river on the Southwark side. Upon a circular
substructure rose two wooden stories, which included the galleries and boxes. These and the
stage were roofed with thatch; the pit or yard was
open to the weather. In the profits of this theatre
Shakespeare was a sharer. Blackfriars Theatre, with
which also Shakespeare's name is associated, was
converted into a building for dramatic performances
from a large house purchased by the elder Burbage

in 1596. The inhabitants of Blackfriars petitioned the privy-council without success against the establishment of the theatre, setting forth in their memorial the various dangers and annoyances to which they would be subjected by its presence in the neighbourhood. For a time it was leased by the Burbages to one Evans for the performances of the boy-actors, Her Majesty's Children of the Chapel. When they quitted it Shakespeare's company took their place, and in the later days of his dramatic career the great poet himself may have appeared on the boards of Blackfriars. Dryden informs us that The Tempest was represented at this theatre and was well received.

§ 15. The theatrical company which produced a play in Elizabethan days had no wish to see the work in print, its publication necessarily detracting from the novelty of the piece. But from the year 1597 onwards several of Shakespeare's dramas were placed in the hands of the booksellers, and were printed, each singly, in quarto form. The first to appear was King Richard II. (1597), from which the deposition scene was omitted. It was speedily followed by King Richard III. A pirated copy of Romeo and Juliet, made up from fragments of manuscript, eked out by notes taken during the performance, and by recollected lines and speeches, appeared in the same year (1597). In 1598 King Henry IV. and the revised version of Love's Labour's Lost were published. Hardly a year, indeed, passed from this date until that of Shakespeare's death without the appearance in quarto of some new tragedy, history, or comedy, or the re-

publication of one which had already issued from
the press. The popularity of Shakespeare's two
chief non-dramatic poems was of remarkable con-
tinuance, as is attested by the number of successive
editions. Occasionally plays or poems by other
writers were foisted on the public by unscrupulous
publishers with the attractive name or initials of
William Shakespeare on the title-page. A list of
his works, most valuable from the light it throws
on their chronology, appears in a "Comparative
Discourse of our English Poets with the Greeke,
Latine, and Italian Poets", which is printed near
the end of a little volume named Palladis Tamia
by Francis Meres, a Master of Arts of both univer-
sities. The chapter was written in the summer of
1598, and it bears remarkable testimony to the high
rank held by Shakespeare both as a narrative and
a dramatic poet. "As the soule of Euphorbus",
says Meres, "was thought to live in Pythagoras, so
the sweete wittie soule of Ovid lives in mellifluous
and honey-tongued Shakespeare; witnes his Venus
and Adonis, his Lucrece, his sugred Sonnets among
his private friends, &c.—As Plautus and Seneca are
accounted the best for comedy and tragedy among
the Latines, so Shakespeare among the English is
the most excellent in both kinds for the stage; for
comedy, witnes his Gentlemen of Verona, his Errors,
his Love labors lost, his Love labours wonne, his
Midsummers night dreame, and his Merchant of
Venice; for tragedy, his Richard the 2, Richard the
3, Henry the 4, King John, Titus Andronicus and
his Romeo and Juliet.—As Epius Stolo said that
the Muses would speake with Plautus tongue, if

they would speak Latin; so I say that the Muses would speak with Shakespeares fine filed phrase, if they would speake English." The Love's Labour's Won which Meres names may be a lost play of Shakespeare, or possibly, as has been conjectured, All's Well that Ends Well in an earlier form may have borne this title. The "sugred Sonnets among his private friends" may be some of those printed afterwards (1609) in the quarto edition of "Shakespeare's Sonnets". Two of these sonnets, with a different text, were included among the poems of The Passionate Pilgrim, 1599, a slender volume made up of pieces of verse, many of which are certainly not by Shakespeare, though his name is placed upon the fraudulent title-page. A theory most skilfully worked out by Mr. Tyler, with some assistance from Mr. Harrison, which identifies the young friend addressed in Shakespeare's Sonnets with William Herbert, afterwards Earl of Pembroke, and the raven-haired lady with Queen Elizabeth's maid of honour, Mistress Mary Fitton, places the first acquaintance of the poet with Herbert, then a youth of eighteen, in the spring of the year 1598. While several other theories of Shakespeare's Sonnets are amusing from their absurdity, this is highly interesting from its ingenuity; and yet it seems to me to remain doubtful whether Herbert and his mistress are in any way connected with these perplexing poems, which endlessly invite the reader and endlessly baffle his attempts to read their biographical meanings clear. Whether Shakespeare formed the acquaintance of William Herbert in this year or not, we may believe that it became memor-

able through the beginning of another friendship,
which, with some possible brief interruption, seems
to have been life-long. In September, 1598, Ben
Jonson's Every Man in his Humour was brought
out by the Lord Chamberlain's company. According to Rowe the comedy was on the point of being
rejected, when Shakespeare, casting his eye over
the manuscript, perceived its merit, and on reading
it through exerted his influence to secure its performance. "I loved the man," wrote Jonson after
the death of Shakespeare, "and do honour his
memory, on this side idolatry, as much as any." It
was inevitable that Jonson, with his classical training and strict ideas on literary style, should be of
the opinion that Shakespeare often wronged his
genius by careless writing: "I remember the players
have often mentioned it as an honour to Shakespeare that, in his writing, whatsoever he penn'd he
never blotted out line. My answer hath been, would
he had blotted a thousand." The noble memorial
verses by Jonson prefixed to the First Folio Shakespeare exalt our poet to a place beside his greatest
predecessors in the literature of Greece and Rome,
and do honour not only to his natural gifts but to
his art. Of the personal relations of the two great
dramatists we have a well-known and delightful
record in Fuller's Worthies, where he tells of their
many wit-combats: "Which two I behold like a
Spanish great galleon and an English man-of-war.
Master Jonson, like the former, was built far higher
in learning, solid, but slow in his performances.
Shakespeare, with the English man-of-war, lesser
in bulk, but lighter in sailing, could turn with all

tides, tack about, and take advantage of all winds by the quickness of his wit and invention."

§ 16. Hours of brilliant wit-combat in the London tavern did not cause Shakespeare to forget his Stratford home. We have seen that in the spring of 1597 he became the purchaser of New Place, a large house standing on nearly an acre of ground. The death of his son Hamnet, in August of the preceding year, left him without male issue; but his purpose to occupy a strong and dignified position in his native town was not turned aside by this grief, which, nevertheless, he must have keenly felt.[1] The draft of a grant of coat-armour to John Shakespeare, dated October, 1596, is in existence. We cannot doubt that the real mover in the matter was John Shakespeare's prosperous son; and the grant not having been made, it was again sought three years later. From 1598 onwards we are to think of the great poet as "William Shakespeare of Stratford-on-Avon, in the county of Warwick, gentleman," although his time was mainly spent in the metropolis or on his professional tours through the provinces. He is returned as holding ten quarters of corn in the Chapel Street Ward of Stratford, in February, 1598. He seems already to have looked forward to enjoying the pleasures of a country life. He laid out part of his garden as a fruit orchard, and at a later date it was he, according to a well-authenticated tradition, who was the first to introduce the mulberry tree among his townsfolk. An

---

[1] Malone supposed that the lamentations of Constance in King John for the loss of her boy may have derived some of their intensity of expression from Shakespeare's personal grief. But King John was probably written before 1596.

attempt was made (1597) by the family towards
the recovery of the mortgaged estate of Asbies, but,
as far as we are aware, without success. Abraham
Sturley of Stratford, writing to his brother-in-law,
Richard Quiney, in London (24th Jan. 1597–98),
mentions that "Mr. Shaksper is willinge to disburse
some monie upon some od yarde land or other at
Shotterie or near about us", and urges his corre-
spondent to move Mr. Shakespeare "to deal in the
matter of our tithes". To purchase this tithe-lease
from the corporation would advantage both Shakespeare and his neighbours: "by the friends he can
make therefor, we think it a fair mark for him to
shoot at;—it obtained would advance him indeed
and would do us much good". "If you bargain
with William Shakespeare," writes Richard Quiney's
father (late in 1598 or early in 1599), "or receive
money therefor, bring your money home that you
may." Richard Quiney was negotiating in the
metropolis matters of importance for the Stratford
Corporation. The only letter addressed to Shakespeare which is known to exist—and it is doubtful
whether the letter was ever delivered—is one from
this Quiney, himself a well-to-do Stratford mercer
(Oct. 1598), asking for a loan of thirty pounds. We
learn at the same time from a letter of Sturley's
(4th Nov. 1598) that Shakespeare had undertaken
to negotiate an advance of money to the corporation. These details are of interest not only as evidence of Shakespeare's growing prosperity and influence, but also as showing that he kept in close
relations with the men of Stratford and had a part
in the public concerns of the town.

§ 17. In the autumn of 1601 Shakespeare lost his father; the funeral took place on September 8th. His widowed mother lived for seven years more, and it was at the same season of the year, and almost to the day, that her death occurred (buried September 9, 1608). John Shakespeare, once the chief burgess of Stratford, had the satisfaction of seeing the fallen fortunes of his family restored through the energy and prudence of his son. An important purchase of land — one hundred and seven acres near Stratford—was made in May, 1602, for which Shakespeare paid the large sum of £320, his brother Gilbert acting in the affair as his agent. A few months later, in September, he added to his possessions a cottage and garden opposite the lower grounds of New Place. His largest purchase was that of July, 1605, when for the sum of £440 he obtained the unexpired term of the moiety of a lease of the tithes of Stratford, Old Stratford, Bishopton, and Welcombe. Twenty acres of pasture were added to his arable land in 1610. The creator of Hamlet and King Lear evidently lived in no dream-world, but had a vigorous grasp of positive fact. A certain Philip Rogers had received bushels of malt from Mr. William Shakespeare to the value of £1, 19s. 10d., and had, moreover, borrowed from him the sum of two shillings. Six shillings had been paid back. But the poet could not see why one pound, fifteen shillings and tenpence due to him should remain in Philip Rogers' pocket, and accordingly he took proceedings (1604) to recover the balance of the debt. Again, in 1608-9 the author of the ardent idealizing Sonnets, published in the latter year, was prosecuting a suit for the recovery of a debt of £6 owed by John Addenbroke, and when a verdict was given for the debt and for costs, Addenbroke not being found within the liberty of the borough, Shakespeare pursued his cause against the debtor's bail, a person named Horneby. It is not always the case that a master in the world of ideas and of imagination is also a master of prudent husbandry in the material world.

The year 1607 was one of mingled joy and sorrow. On June the 5th Shakespeare's eldest daughter, Susanna, was married in Stratford-on-Avon to Mr. John Hall, a Master of Arts and a successful physician. The bride was twenty-five years of age; the bridegroom thirty-two. So midsummer had its rejoicings; but December closed darkly, for it was on the last day of 1607 that the great bell of St. Saviour's, Southwark, tolled for the burial of Shakespeare's brother Edmund. A few weeks later and Shakespeare had attained, before the age of forty-four, the dignity of being a grandfather; Elizabeth, the only daughter of the Halls, was born in February, 1608, and her baby presence must have cheered the few short remaining months of the life of Shakespeare's mother. It seems probable that he continued to reside in Stratford for a little while after his mother's funeral, for on October 16th he stood as godfather at the baptism of William Walker, the child of a mercer and alderman of the town; to this godchild he afterwards bequeathed "twenty shillings in gold".

§ 18. At what precise date Shakespeare retired

from the theatre and sold his shares in the Globe cannot be ascertained. It was probably not earlier than 1611, not later than 1613. In March, 1613, he bought for £140 a house in London near the Blackfriars Theatre, £60 of the purchase money remaining on mortgage. Mr. Halliwell-Phillipps supposes that Shakespeare may have intended to convert part of the house, the ground-floor of which had been a haberdasher's shop, into his town residence, and that at the date of the purchase he was still connected with the stage. But all that we certainly know is that before his death he leased this London house to John Robinson, who, as Halliwell-Phillipps notices, "was oddly enough, one of the persons who had violently opposed the establishment of the neighbouring theatre". In midsummer of the year 1613 the Globe Theatre was destroyed by fire, "while Burbage's company were acting the play of Henry VIII., and there shooting off certain chambers in the way of triumph" (T. Lorkin's letter to Sir T. Puckering). This Henry VIII. was not improbably the play which, with certain alterations, we possess among Shakespeare's works, and which is partly from his hand. It is possible that many manuscripts of dramatists—including some by Shakespeare — perished in the flames. The Globe was rebuilt in a costlier manner, and was opened in 1614; but the stage on which the greatest dramatic works in all literature had been first presented had ceased to exist, and their author, like his own wise Prospero, had broken his magic staff and put off his robes of enchantment.

§ 19. We know little of Shakespeare's elder days

at Stratford. "The latter part of his life," says
Rowe, "was spent, as all men of good sense will
wish theirs may be, in ease, retirement, and the
conversation of his friends. . . . His pleasur-
able wit and good-nature engaged him in the acquaintance and entitled him to the friendship of
the gentlemen of the neighbourhood." Amongst
his acquaintances was John Combe, who, dying in
1614, left him a legacy of £5. A satirical epitaph
on Combe, said to have been produced impromptu
by Shakespeare, has been handed down by tradition; but there is little evidence to show that the
lines are genuine. In the autumn of the same year
an attempt was made to inclose a portion of the
neighbouring common-fields. It is not quite certain whether Shakespeare endeavoured to forward
(as Halliwell-Phillipps maintains) or to oppose the
project; there is no doubt that he took measures
to secure himself against loss if the inclosure should
be effected.[1] An entry of 1614 in the accounts of
the Stratford Chamberlain sets our fancy pleasantly
to work. "Item: For one quart of sack, and one
quart of clarett wine, given to a preacher at the
New Place xxd." Stratford had grown puritanical
since Shakespeare was a boy; in 1602, and again
in 1612, orders against plays and interludes were
made by the corporation; at last the players were
paid *not* to perform. "Mrs. Hall and her husband",
as I have elsewhere written, "did not forfeit the

[1] The words in the diary of Thomas Greene, town-clerk of Stratford,
commonly printed "Mr. Shakspeare tellyng J. Greene that he was
not able to bear the encloseing of Welcombe", seem in fact to be
"that I was not able", &c. Dr. Ingleby supposed that Greene wrote
"I" by mistake.

poet's regard because they were somewhat puri-
tanically inclined.   Perhaps Shakespeare's wife had
sought in religion a satisfaction which her marriage
had not afforded.   We can imagine the great interpreter of life listening with a serious smile to the
whole truth as expounded by the preacher, and re-
cognizing as a pleasant human foible the preacher's
interest in claret and sherry sack."   If there were
any truth in the crab-tree legend (which, however,
dates only from 1762) we should believe that Shakespeare himself, with the encouragement of his companion Ben Jonson, could for the nonce carouse
"potations pottle-deep", and become somewhat
more than flustered with his cups.

In February, 1616, Shakespeare saw Judith, his
second daughter, married.   Her husband, Thomas
Quiney, a son of the Richard Quiney who had
begged Shakespeare for a loan of money, was four
years younger than his wife.   He was certainly a
fairly educated man, and during the earlier portion
of his married life he occupied a good position in
the town, doing business as a vintner, and becoming
a member of the corporation and subsequently their
chamberlain.   But after a time prosperity forsook
him, and he drifted to London.   His eldest son,
named Shakespeare Quiney, died an infant; two
younger sons, Richard and Thomas, reached manhood, but both died childless before their mother,
who lived on through the Civil War to Restoration
days.   She died in 1662 in her seventy-eighth year.

§ 20. Before the marriage took place—a marriage
celebrated somewhat hastily without a license—
Shakespeare, then in perfect health, had given in-

structions for his will. The draft copy was ready for engrossment, but the fair copy had not yet been made when in March, 1616, the testator was taken seriously ill. Delay in obtaining the necessary signatures was deemed inexpedient, and certain corrections having been made by interlineation the draft copy was duly signed by the sick man and the witnesses. The chief part of his property was left to his eldest daughter, but Judith received a substantial sum of money; his sister Joan Hart, who became a widow a few days before her brother's death, was considerately remembered; small sums were left to the sons of his sister; ten pounds to the poor of Stratford; nor did Shakespeare as he lay mortally ill forget his former fellows of the Globe Theatre, for to Richard Burbage, John Hemmings, and Henry Condell he left, by an interlineation, "twenty-six shillings and eight pence a-piece to buy them ringes". Beside the signatures at the foot of each page the words "by me" at the close of the will are in Shakespeare's handwriting, and no other words, except his own name, remain to us in the poet's autograph. On Tuesday, April 23, 1616, the great spirit, "a little lower than the angels", passed away.[1]

The malady of which Shakespeare died is sup-

[1] The name of Shakespeare is found written in a copy of Florio's Montaigne purchased for £100 by the British Museum in 1838. Its genuineness has been disputed. The words "Wllm Shakspeare, hundred and twenty poundes" are written on a paper found in the original binding of a copy of North's Plutarch, 1603, now in the Boston (U.S.A.) Public Library. There are many reasons in favour of its genuineness, but they are not decisive. It is not suggested that the volume ever belonged to Shakespeare. See Bulletin of the Boston Public Library, vol. 8. no. 4.

posed to have been a fever. According to the memoranda-book written in 1662–63 by the Rev. John Ward, vicar of Stratford-on-Avon, it was contracted after a "merry meeting" with Drayton and Ben Jonson, at which the convivial friends "drank too hard". We may perhaps agree with Halliwell-Phillipps in finding a sufficient cause for blood-poisoning in the wretched sanitary conditions surrounding New Place. "If truth, and not romance, is to be invoked," says this careful biographer, "were there the woodbine and sweet honeysuckle within reach of the poet's death-bed, their fragrance would have been neutralized by their vicinity to middens, fetid water-courses, mud-walls, and piggeries."

On April 25th Shakespeare's body was laid in its resting-place, the chancel of the parish church, to which position for a grave the owner of the tithes had an acknowledged right. The grave is near the north wall of the chancel. Over the spot where the body lies was placed a slab bearing the inscription, which a tradition attributes to Shakespeare himself:—

> GOOD FREND FOR IESUS SAKE FORBEARE
> TO DIGG THE DVST ENCLOASED HEARE;
> BLESTE BE THE MAN THAT SPARES THES STONES,
> AND CVRST BE HE THAT MOVES MY BONES.

"It should be remembered", observes Halliwell-Phillipps, "that the transfer of bones from graves to the charnel-house was then an ordinary practice at Stratford-on-Avon." Shakespeare's bones have lain more secure in their modest grave during three centuries than those of Schiller in the grand-ducal vault at Weimar.

§ 21. Shakespeare's widow lived for more than seven years after her husband's death. She died on August 6th, 1623. The Halls continued to reside at New Place; the physician attained a high reputation for skill in his profession; in matters of faith he seems to have inclined more decidedly to Puritanism as the years went by. His death took place in 1635; that of his wife, Susanna Hall—who was esteemed for her goodness, piety, and bright intelligence — in 1649. Elizabeth Hall, Shakespeare's grandchild, was twice married; on April 22, 1626, to Thomas Nash, who died in 1647; and secondly, about two years after, to Sir John Barnard of Abington, in the county of Northampton. She had no child by either husband, and on her death, in February 1669–70, the lineal descent from Shakespeare came to an end.

Not long after his death, certainly before 1623, a monument was erected to Shakespeare on the northern wall of the chancel of the parish church at Stratford. It contains a life-sized bust, the work either of Gerard Johnson, sculptor and "tombemaker", a native of Amsterdam who resided in London, or of Johnson's son. The bust—a somewhat coarse piece of art—is made of a soft bluish limestone; several excellent judges are of opinion that it was cut from a death-mask as model. It presents a face powerful and full-blooded, rather than refined or subtle; the great dome of the forehead is, however, a very striking feature. Originally the bust was coloured to resemble life; the eyes a light hazel, the hair and beard auburn, the doublet scarlet, and the sleeveless gown worn over

it black.   The right hand holds a pen, the left
rests on a sheet of paper placed upon a cushion.
Underneath the cushion is the following inscription :—

IVDICIO PYLIUM, GENIO SOCRATEM, ARTE MARONEM,
TERRA TEGIT, POPVLVS MÆRET, OLYMPUS HABET.

STAY PASSENGER, WHY GOEST THOV BY SO FAST?
READ IF THOV CANST, WHOM ENVIOUS DEATH HATH PLAST,
WITH IN THIS MONVMENT. SHAKSPEARE: WITH WHOME
QVICK NATVRE DIDE: WHOSE NAME DOTH DECK Yˢ TOMBE,
FAR MORE THAN COST: SIEH ALL, Yᵀ HE HATH WRITT,
LEAVES LIVING ART, BVT PAGE, TO SERVE HIS WITT.

OBIIT ANNO DOⁱ 1616.
ÆTATIS 53 DIE 23 AP.

In 1793, on the advice of Edmond Malone, the
bust was painted white; and so it remained until
1861, when it was recoloured as at the first. Beside
the Stratford bust there is only one unquestionable
portrait of the great poet—that upon the title-page
of the First Folio (1623). It was engraved by
Martin Droeshout, and verses by Ben Jonson commend it as a trustworthy likeness. It is ill executed,
yet it seems to me a more pleasing portrait than
the bust, while there is enough in common between
the two to assure us that in each there is at least
something of the substance of truth. The authenticity of the celebrated Kesselstadt death-mask is
very doubtful, but we could wish to believe that
this noble and refined face was indeed that of
Shakespeare. The Chandos, the Felton, the Jansen,
and the Stratford portraits are all of questionable
pedigree; many other alleged likenesses can be
proved to be forgeries. We must be content to
accept certain broad facts from the bust and the
Droeshout print, and supply from our imagination

the spirit and the life which these unfortunately
lack. And if this should leave us at the last un-
satisfied we may be well content to follow the
counsel of Ben Jonson:

> Reader, looke
> Not on his Picture, but his Booke.

II.

§ 22. Studying Shakespeare's Book of Might, as
Jonson exhorts us to do, we assuredly make acquaintance with the man in the best possible way;
we are constantly in contact with his mind; he
neighbours us on every side, rouses our intellect,
moves our passions, confirms our will, moulds our
character, touches our spirit to finer issues, envelops
us with the atmosphere of his wisdom, courage,
mirth, benignity. We breathe his influence. And
yet so effectually does he hide himself behind his
creation, that even while we live and move in his
power and presence, it seems as if we knew him
not and could never know him aright. Let us take
heart; he who knows the offspring of Shakespeare's
genius knows the man, and indeed is far more inti-
mate with Shakespeare's mind than if he were to
meet the great poet now and again in the tiring-
room of the Globe, or the inner chamber of the
Mermaid Tavern, or even in the quietude of his
Stratford fields and lanes.

Shakespeare was fortunate in the moment of his
advent to the stage. The English people had suc-
cessfully passed through a period of probation, and
now stood "upon the top of happy hours". The

classical culture of the Renaissance and its passionate temper had been united in the national mind with the grave thought and the moral earnestness of the Reformation. The fires of Smithfield were extinct; the conspiracies against the queen had been defeated; the Spanish fleet had been flung from our inviolable shores. A spirit of unbounded energy was abroad, with an exultant patriotic pride and an exhilarating consciousness of power. It was a great age of action, and men through their imagination were swift to enter into all that great deeds spring from—high thoughts, ardent desires, fierce indignation, fervent love. Life in every form and aspect was infinitely interesting to them. And if they saw and felt the tragic side of things, none the less did they enjoy the comedy of human existence. Its laughter and its tears were alike near and real for them, and one of these, as they felt, could easily pass into the other.

The moment was especially a fortunate one for a dramatic writer. The development of every art during its earlier stages is gradual and slow; the bud insensibly swells and matures, then suddenly some genial morning the calyx bursts, the bud becomes a blossom, and all its colour and fragrance are open to the day. So it was with the dramatic art in the later Elizabethan years. Its history from the earliest miracle-plays had been one of some centuries. The drama was not the creation of a few eminent individuals, but rather a product of the national mind distinguished by the features of the national character. In the Collective Mystery, which surveyed the history of the human race from the origin of man to the judgment-day, it had gained an epic breadth. In the Moralities it had acquired an ethical depth, a seriousness of moral purpose, and this didactic tendency had in a measure been saved from the aridity and abstractedness of mere allegory by the close connection of the Morality with historical passions, persons, and events. In both the Miracles and the Moralities scope had been found for the play of humour, some- times deliberately sought as a relief from the poetry of edification, sometimes naively mingling with passages of grace, tenderness, or pathos, and en- hancing the effect of these. Under the influence of a growing sense of art, aided by classical models, and Italian plays and tales of passion and of wit, the elder forms of the English drama passed away or were transmuted into regular tragedy, comedy, and history. The mirth was still often rude, but it began to be organized around some dramatic centre, and to find its sources not merely in ridiculous incidents, but in what is mirth-provoking in human character. The terror and pity were often coarsely stimulated by scenes of outrage and inexhaustible effusion of blood; but amid these scenes of horror figures which had in them at least great tragic possibilities sometimes appeared. Perhaps the most truly English of the several dramatic forms was the Chronicle History, allied at once with tragedy and comedy, but in some degree saved from the extra- vagances of each by the substantial matter of historical fact with which it dealt. When great deeds were actually accomplished by Englishmen they had a ready credence of the imagination for the heroic achievements of their ancestors as set forth in these Histories. They had even some of the elements of a true historic sense.

§ 23. Shakespeare's immediate predecessors in the drama were scholar-poets, who yet, with one exception—that of John Lyly—may be said to have used popular methods, and to have made their appeal not to scholarly or courtly spectators, but to the public. As poets of the Renaissance they delighted in classical allusion and classical imagery, but these served chiefly as a colour and varnish of their art; in conception it was essentially romantic and English of the Elizabethan days. The tragedies of Marlowe in their plots are pure melodrama, but the melodrama is glorified by the genius of a poet who was a lofty idealist in art, and whose imagination hungered and thirsted after beauty. In each of his earlier plays a great protagonist stands forth who is the incarnation of some supreme passion; Tamburlaine, embodying the mere lust of sway in its crudest form; Barrabas, the passion of avarice with attendant power; Faustus, the desire of boundless knowledge with the empire that knowledge brings. In Edward II. the dramatist gave the model of a noble historical play, from which Shakespeare perhaps made studies in writing scenes of his own Richard II. Comedy owed nearly as much to Greene and Peele as tragedy owed to Marlowe. They first lifted comedy out of its mean surroundings and made it poetical. Not that they despised buffooneries and horseplay as modes of raising a laugh, but they did not rest content with these.

Amid the sordid haunts and coarse excesses of his
London life Greene had an imagination which delighted in the beauty and innocence of the country-
side and rural pleasures, real or Arcadian; in the
company of knaves and trulls he could conceive,
as no other dramatist of his time, the purity and
sweetness of English wife and maiden. From each
of his predecessors Shakespeare gained something
for his art, and he quickly surpassed them all.
From Marlowe he learnt the use of that majestic
measure, blank verse, first heard on a public stage
in the tragedy of Tamburlaine; and it became
ductile in his hands and capable of infinite variety.
From Greene he learnt the use of the rhymed
couplet, which he employed with such happy facility
in his earlier plays. Kyd it may have been who
instructed him in various pieces of rhetorical sleight
of hand in verse, which could be adapted to the
expression of dramatic passion or to the control of
that expression. The prose of lively dialogue, with
quick turns of wit and repartee, which we find in the
first comedies of Shakespeare, was in large measure
derived from Lyly.

§ 24. In all that is external and mechanical
the theatre was still comparatively rude. During
Shakespeare's connection with the stage the buildings used for dramatic entertainments were of two
classes—public theatres, and those which were
called private. The private theatres were the
smaller in size, and were wholly roofed in, whereas
the public theatres, except over the stage and
boxes, were open to the sky. In private theatres
the performances commonly took place by the

light of candles or cressets; in public theatres, by
daylight. In both the play began in the afternoon,
often at three o'clock, and ended at five or between
five and six o'clock. The spectators who occupied
the pit or "yard" were obliged in public theatres to
stand; in private theatres they were seated. The
interior form of theatres was usually circular or
oval, and the boxes or "rooms" and galleries or
"scaffolds" rose above one another in tiers as they
do at present. The prices for admittance to various
houses and to various parts of the house ranged
from one penny or twopence to two shillings or
half-a-crown. In public theatres young men of
rank and fashion were accommodated with stools
on each side of the rush-strewn stage, where their
attendants waited upon them and supplied them
with their pipes of tobacco. Ladies visiting the
theatre sometimes wore masks. Movable painted
scenery had not yet been devised; but stage pro-
perties, some of which served as elements of scenery,
were numerous; rocks and tombs, stairs and
steeples, banks and bay-trees, are enumerated in
an old inventory. Costumes were often rich and
costly. In front of the stage ran curtains which
could be drawn and withdrawn as was needful, and
at the back of the stage similar curtains, named
"traverses", occupied the place of our scenery, and
could be used for exits and entrances of actors.
When a tragedy was represented the stage was
sometimes hung with black. Towards the rear of
the stage rose an upper stage, from which, when it
seemed suitable, part of the dialogue could be
spoken. This upper stage might be imagined the

walls of a besieged city as in King John, or a
balcony as in Romeo and Juliet, or a stage within
the stage as in the play-scene of Hamlet. The
opening of the play was announced by three sound-
ings or flourishes of the trumpet; during its performance a flag displayed from the roof informed
the public in the streets that entertainment was
provided for them within. A player wearing a
black velvet cloak delivered the prologue. In the
intervals of acting the band, stationed below at
the side of the stage, helped to beguile the time.
Occasionally an epilogue was pronounced; we find
that such was the case with As You Like It, where
the epilogue is spoken by Rosalind in prose, and
The Tempest, where it is spoken by Prospero in
verse. A prayer for the reigning monarch, recited
by the actors kneeling on the stage, closed the
piece. But this devout exercise was often immediately preceded or followed by the clown's
"jig", a humorous or burlesque effusion in verse,
often rhymed, which the merryman sang, sometimes dancing while he sang, to the accompaniment
of pipe and tabor. It must be remembered as one
of the most important differences between the
Elizabethan stage and the stage subsequent to the
Restoration of King Charles II., that in the earlier
period female parts were taken by boys. " By 'r
lady," says Hamlet to the growing youth who acted
the Player Queen, "your ladyship is nearer to
heaven than when I saw you last, by the altitude of
a chopine. Pray God, your voice, like a piece of
uncurrent gold, be not cracked within the ring."
And among the possible indignities on which the

imagination of the Egyptian queen dwells is that of
being presented by the comedians on the stage,
where some "squeaking Cleopatra" might "boy
her greatness". We can well believe that Shakespeare would have rejoiced if it were possible to
intrust such parts as those of Cleopatra, Lady
Macbeth, Juliet, Rosalind, Viola, Imogen, to an
actress of genius, capable of entering into all his
meanings, instead of to a performer of the other
sex, "not old enough for a man, nor young enough
for a boy; as a squash is before 't is a peascod, or a
codling when 't is almost an apple". Nor can we
suppose that he was contented with the scanty
resources of the Elizabethan theatre, or thought its
poverty an advantage to his art. In the Prologue
to King Henry V. he apologizes for the very inadequate representation of great historical events,
and appeals to the imagination of the spectators to
supply the deficiencies of the stage.

A rude sketch of the interior of the Swan Theatre,
London, as it was about the year 1596, was not long
since brought to light in the University Library,
Utrecht. It is from the hand of a learned Dutch-
man, Johannes de Witt, who visited England towards
the close of the reign of Elizabeth.[1] The stage,
strongly supported on timber bulks, is occupied by
three actors, and has for all its furniture a bench on
which a female figure is seated. Neither curtains
nor traverses appear. At the back of the stage,
which is open to the weather, is the tiring-room, to
which two doors give entrance, and above this rises

[1] See Zur Kenntnis der Altenglischen Bühne, by Karl Theodore
Gaedertz (Bremen, 1888).

a covered balcony or row of boxes occupied by spectators, but available at need for the actors.

Sketch of the Interior of the Swan Theatre.

The trumpeter is seen at the door of a covered chamber near the gallery-roof, and from its summit floats a flag having upon it the figure of a swan.

The form of the building is oval. No other draw-
ing of the interior of an Elizabethan theatre is
known to exist.

§ 25. Assuming that Shakespeare, after the
alleged deer-stealing adventure, left Stratford for
London in 1586 or 1587, we can hardly suppose
that any of the work which has come down to us
was written before 1589. He had much to learn,
which could not be learnt in a day. At a considerably later date he was still a workman in his
apprenticeship to the dramatic craft, engaged in
rehandling the work of Greene and Marlowe. He
continued to write for the stage until 1611 or perhaps 1613. Thus his entire career as a dramatist
covers some twenty or at most five-and-twenty
years. Various attempts have been made by
Shakespeare scholars to distinguish the successive
stages in the development of his genius, and to
classify his plays in a series of chronological groups.
The latest attempt is that of a learned French
Orientalist, who is also a well-informed student of
English literature, M. James Darmesteter. It is
substantially identical with that which I had myself
proposed, a division of the total twenty or twenty-
five years of Shakespeare's authorship into four
periods of unequal length, to which I had given
names intended to lay hold of the student's memory,
names which, without being fanciful, should be
striking and easy to bear in mind. The earliest
period I called "In the Workshop", meaning by
this the term of apprenticeship and tentative effort.
The years which immediately followed, during
which Shakespeare, though a master of his art,

dwelt much on the broad surface of human life, years represented by the best English histories and some of the brightest comedies, I named " In the World ". To indicate the third period, that of the serious, dark, or bitter comedies, and those great tragedies in which the poet makes his searching inquisition into evil, the title " Out of the Depths " served sufficiently well. Finally, for the closing period, when the romantic comedies, at once grave and glad—Cymbeline, The Winter's Tale, The Tempest—were written, I chose the name " On the Heights ", signifying thereby that in these exquisite plays Shakespeare had attained an altitude from which he saw human life in a clear and solemn vision, looking down through a pellucid atmosphere upon human joys and sorrows with a certain aloofness or disengagement, yet at the same time with a tender and pathetic interest. The names adopted by M. Darmesteter may, if the reader chooses, replace those which I ventured to offer, only the reader should be on his guard against the notion that at any time either what we now term " pessimism " or what we term " optimism " formed the creed, or any portion of the creed, of Shakespeare. According to M. Darmesteter the first period extends from 1588 to 1593; he names it " Les Années d'Apprentissage "; it is succeeded by the " Période d'Épanouissement " (1593-1601); upon which follows the " Période Pessimiste " (1601-8); and the great career closes with the rolling away of clouds and the outbeaming of a serene sun in the " Période Optimiste " (1608-13).

§ 26. In the study of the chronology of Shakespeare's plays the larger results may be considered as certain. Much was done long since to determine the order of the plays by Malone. The dates of the publication of the early quartos, the dates of the entries of plays in the registers of the Stationers' Company, mention of the plays, or allusion to them or quotations from them, in contemporary writings, references in the plays themselves to recent historical events or incidents of the day, quotations made by Shakespeare from books of known date—evidence of these various kinds had accumulated long since in the hands of students of the drama, and had sufficed to ascertain the Shakespearian chronology at least in outline. The internal evidence derived from the changes of the dramatist's style and diction, passing from the studious elaborateness of such a play as The Two Gentlemen of Verona to the subtlety in swiftness of utterance in such a play as The Tempest, came to the aid of evidence that was wholly or in part external. If classical allusions were crowded and often inappropriate, if puns and forced conceits were frequent, if the expression of strong feeling swelled into bombast, it was easy to perceive that the play must be of an early or comparatively early date. If the structure of the play and the grouping of the characters were stiff and symmetrical, it could hardly belong to the later stages of Shakespeare's authorship. If the characterization were faint or over-broad, if the thoughts on human life were slight and superficial, if the wit was verbal and shallow, if the humour was unmingled with pathos, again we might infer that the work was one of the poet's earlier years.

No one who read the Comedy of Errors and Measure for Measure could suppose that they lay near one another in point of time; no one could suppose that Romeo and Juliet, full of true passion and beauty as it is, could be followed without a great interval by Antony and Cleopatra. In recent years the study of changes which Shakespeare's versification underwent has in a striking manner confirmed the results previously attained, and perhaps has added something to them. As he grew to be a master of his craft the poet came to feel that rhyme rather interrupted than aided the expression of dramatic feeling; having employed rhyme at first freely, and then with reserve, he finally discarded it altogether. At the same time his blank verse underwent various changes, which may all be summed up in the general statement that it became less mechanical and more vital, less formally regular and more swift, subtle and complex—complex not with the intricacy of mechanical arrangement but with the mystery and the movement of life. The flow of the verse became freer; it paused less frequently at the close of the line; it ran into subtly modulated periods; it adapted itself to the expression of every varying mood of feeling; it overleaped the allotted ten syllables, or gathered itself up into a narrower space as the movement of passion required; it was no longer the decorated raiment but rather the living body of the idea.

§ 27. Shakespeare's years of apprenticeship produced tentative work of the most various kinds, and constantly growing in excellence of handling. Although himself no classical scholar, in the higher sense of that word, and but slightly, if at all, acquainted at first hand with Italian literature, his early plays and poems exhibit the Renaissance influences derived from classical themes, Latin models in tragedy and comedy, and the glad-coloured or sad-coloured literature of the south. "Titus Andronicus," writes an excellent critic, "in many of its characteristic features, reflects the form of Roman tragedy almost universally accepted and followed in the earlier period of the drama. . . . The Medea and Thyestes of Seneca are crowded with Pagan horrors of the most revolting kind. It is true these horrors are usually related, not represented, although in the Medea the maddened heroine kills her children on the stage. But from these tragedies the conception of the physically horrible as an element of tragedy was imported into the early English drama, and intensified by the realistic tendency which the events of the time and the taste of their ruder audiences had impressed upon the common stages." With respect to Titus Andronicus, however, we must remember that, in all probability, Shakespeare is not responsible for its horrors and shames. He may possibly have begun his worldly career as a butcher's apprentice at Stratford-on-Avon. We are not compelled to believe that his dramatic career opened in the slaughter-house. If, to aid his theatrical fellows, he retouched the old play of Titus Andronicus, he certainly took no pleasure in lopped limbs and the reek of blood. If for an hour he was brought into contact with the tragedy of gross and material horror, it was only that he might turn away from it for ever. Whether he wrote a few lines of the play here and a few lines there, or wrote them not, concerns us but little; the play taken as a whole may justly be described as of the pre-Shakespearian school.

The influence of Latin comedy is seen in the Comedy of Errors. While the main subject was derived from the Menæchmi of Plautus, some hints were also taken from his Amphitruo. But if Seneca was too heavy for Shakespeare, Plautus was somewhat too light. Our dramatist, indeed, complicates the plot and diversifies the mirthful entanglements, making the fun fly faster by adding to the twin-brothers Antipholus their twin-attendants Dromio. But he adds also a serious background, and towards the close he rises for a little space from mirth to pathos. The ingenious construction of the play, its skilful network of incidents, its bright intricacy which never falls into confusion are remarkable, for Shakespeare is commonly credited with having paid but little attention to his plots.

Love's Labour's Lost may be earlier in date than the Comedy of Errors. It was perhaps the first independent play of Shakespeare's authorship, but, as we have received it, the work, considerably altered from the original version, is a recast of the year 1598. Gervinus has remarked that the tone of the Italian school prevails here more than in any other play: "In the burlesque parts of Love's Labour's Lost we meet with two favourite characters or caricatures of the Italian comedy; the Pedant, that is the schoolmaster and grammarian, and the military Braggart, the Thraso of the Latin, the 'Captain

Spavento' of the Italian stage". Shakespeare, however, did not merely reproduce dramatic types or
stock figures; he had his eye on the affectations
and mannerisms of his own day. It is as if some-
one of our generation were to make his début by a
theatrical satire on the so-called æsthetes of a few
years since, with skits at our fashionable scientific
pedantry, our woman's-rights movement, and other
admired modes of the time. There is in Love's
Labour 's Lost an impatience of folly, dulness, and
ineptitude which is a happy symptom of youth.
Something of the writer's youthful philosophy also
appears in the play; it is a dramatic plea against
shaping our lives by narrow rules and artificial sys-
tems. Let us not confine ourselves within a pale
of petty regulations—such is Shakespeare's teach-
ing—but rather launch forth into the world, and
have faith in that broad wisdom or good sense
which comes by natural methods, a wisdom won
through joy and pain, through frank dealing with
our fellows, through the lore of life and love. In
certain speeches of Biron we seem to hear the
authentic voice of the youthful Shakespeare.

The Comedy of Errors is a comedy of incidents
—almost a farce ; Love's Labour 's Lost is a comedy
of dialogue; in The Two Gentlemen of Verona
Shakespeare made his first essay in what we may
call romantic narrative comedy. The scene is Italy,
the land of romance for the imagination of Elizabethan England. Some of the incidents seem to
be derived from a Spanish pastoral romance and
some from a tale by Bandello. Love and friendship and their mutual relations form the general

theme. The play is the harbinger of some of the most exquisite of the later comedies, and contains a series of sketches which were afterwards worked up into finished pictures. Julia in her male disguise announces, as it were, the more graceful disguisers Viola and Rosalind, Portia and Imogen. The wit combats of clowns have a fascination for Shakespeare or for his audience, but in Launce appears something better—the first of those vulgar humorists who enrich the stage with so much of mirth and the wisdom of mirth, and lacking whom the garden in Illyria and the glades of Arden would appear half-desolate. The Two Gentlemen of Verona would seem to have been written with careful elaboration; the characters are arranged so as to balance each other with a somewhat artificial regularity; the imagery and versification are studiously wrought. The defects of the plot arise perhaps from the fact that it was the author's first experiment in what I have termed romantic narrative comedy. He was not yet a master in the art of construction; if the subject favoured him the plot of a play might be excellent; if it did not favour him, the scenes might hang somewhat loosely together.

Another experiment, and in an altogether different direction, was made in A Midsummer Night's Dream. It is in part a perfect piece of lyrical poetry, in part a very imperfect drama. The characterization of the lovers is faint and pale; their quarrels and reconciliations interest us little; they are indeed invented to be the sport of accident, and so cannot be strongly drawn. But the fairy poetry was a new and exquisite creation in English literature; and the English stage had previously possessed no group of humorous figures to compare with that formed by "sweet bully Bottom" and his compeers. The scene is again classic ground, and the time is that of classical antiquity; but the spirit of the play is essentially romantic. Theseus is a great mediæval knight or an Elizabethan noble; his Amazonian bride Hippolyta might as well be some gracious English châtelaine. Everything in the play mingles with its opposite in dream-like fashion —the modern and the antique, London and Athens, the moonlight elves and the rude mechanicals, the jests of fairyland and the vexations of mortal lovers, fancy and frolic, magnificence and grotesqueness, drollery and romance.

§ 28. Of these early comedies in which Shakespeare was experimenting in various directions, no one is quite a dramatic masterpiece. Evidences of the 'prentice hand appear in each—here in tediousness of dialogue, here in artificial arrangement of the figures, here in faulty construction of the plot, here in feebleness of characterization, here in languor of style, and here in undramatic development of the imagery. But each of these plays contains something admirable, something which no writer of the time except Shakespeare could have created; taken together they make up a great achievement for a poet's early years, and give unmistakable prediction of the higher work which is to follow. It is worth noting how often in this first group of comedies the mirth is derived not from the deeper things of the spirit, but from odd surprises, mistakes of identity, disguisings, bewilderments, and confusion; in a word, from what is external and accidental rather than from what is intimately related with character.

In A Midsummer Night's Dream the lyrical poet in Shakespeare more nearly overmatches the dramatist than in any other of his plays. In Venus and Adonis and Lucrece the dramatist causes some embarrassment to the narrative poet. Shakespeare's endeavour in the earlier of the two is first to paint in the manner of an artist of the Renaissance a glowing picture of the enamoured Queen of Love; and secondly, to invent elaborate speeches for his two chief personages in that style of high-wrought fantasy which was the fashion of the time. He succeeded in his endeavour, and the poem delighted a generation of young readers. But the Venus and Adonis has all the errors of a poet's early work and all the vices of the Elizabethan style. It is full of florid beauties; it is infinitely sweet in its versification; but ingenuity too often replaces passion, and the narrative is perpetually checked by elaborate exercises of fancy. The companion poem Lucrece reverses the motive of the Venus; in the Venus feminine passion strives against boyish coldness; in Lucrece it is a man who makes his assault on womanly chastity. Deep notes are sounded by the poet, radiant heights are touched; but he cannot in these poems transcend the manner of his age. He follows rather than leads. Having made these brilliant essays in a province not properly his own, Shakespeare, notwithstanding the popularity of both poems, seems to have recognized the fact that here his genius could not find its true sphere, and he never again attempted the miniature epic.

§ 29. While engaged on his early comedies Shakespeare was also at work on historical tragedy. But here he attained artistic independence only by degrees, and at first he was manifestly in tutelage to his great predecessor Marlowe. The authorship of the first part of Henry VI. is not ascertained; it probably received additions from Shakespeare's hand; but we may say of this play, as we have said of Titus Andronicus, that it is essentially pre-Shakespearian. In the Second and Third Parts of Henry VI. the work of Shakespeare is found side by side with that of Marlowe, and the pupil proved himself so apt that it is a matter of extreme difficulty to distinguish his contributions from those of the master. The younger poet had much to learn from the mighty wielder of blank verse who has poured into the English drama the life-blood of passion and an unquenchable ardour of imagination. In the tragedy of King Richard III. Shakespeare completed the tetralogy of the house of York, and he sustained and even developed the Marlowesque style of the earlier dramas. "This only of all Shakespeare's plays", says Mr. Swinburne, "belongs absolutely to the school of Marlowe. The influence of the elder master, and that influence alone, is perceptible from end to end. . . . It is as fiery in passion, as single in purpose, as rhetorical often though never so inflated in expression, as Tamburlaine itself." The protagonist, as in the tragedies of Marlowe, is thrust forward and dominates the whole play. Its opening is in the manner of Marlowe—an exordium in the form of a soliloquy.

The tetralogy of the House of Lancaster opens

with King Richard II. Whether that play was
chronologically a little earlier or a little later than
King Richard III. we shall do well to group the
three parts of King Henry VI. with King Richard
III., connected as they are by their subject, and
closely related by their Marlowesque style. King
Richard II., it seems to me, while historically the
first of the series of plays which is continued in
King Henry IV. and King Henry V., in point of
style, and perhaps also in the date of its production, lies close to King John. In both plays Shakespeare has almost entirely delivered himself from
the influence of Marlowe, though some scenes of
King Richard II. were not written without a vivid
recollection of passages in Marlowe's English historical drama. In both plays Shakespeare seems
to be feeling after a way of his own—that manner
which was perfected in King Henry IV.; in both
plays rhyme is freely used, much more freely, however, in King Richard II., which is certainly earlier
in the chronological order than King John; from
both plays prose is absent. The subjects are not
historically connected; King John stands apart
from both the Lancastrian and the Yorkist series.
But there is this in common between King John
and King Richard II., that in each the dramatist
studies the ruin of his country as caused by evil or
incompetent rule, and in each he sounds some of
those trumpet-notes of patriotic enthusiasm which
must have echoed gloriously in the hearts of men
who had witnessed the recent overthrow of the Ar-
mada. The poet does not often deal in mere pane-
gyric of his native land, and he can smile humor-

ously at the foibles of his countrymen; he doubtless
felt that it is the part of a genuine patriot to make
keen inquisition into the sources of national disaster
and defection.   But twice or three times his pride
and joy in the glorious land of his birth must have
an outbreak:

> Come the three corners of the world in arms
> And we shall shock them.   Nought shall make us rue,
> If England to itself do rest but true.

With such a trumpet-note King John closes.   And
amid Gaunt's prophetic fears upon his death-bed
appears the vision of England as it had been and
might be again—

> This royal throne of kings, this scepter'd isle,
> This earth of majesty, this seat of Mars,
> This other Eden, demi-Paradise,
> This blessed spot, the earth, this realm, this England.

In King John the feebleness of foreign policy, in
King Richard II. the vices of domestic government
are censured.   In each play individual strength and
courage are honoured; in King John the hope of
England centres in the person of Cœur de Lion's
bastard son, a mediæval John Bull cased in armour;
in King Richard II. such salvation as is possible
must come from the aspiring Bolingbroke, "one
still strong man in a blatant land".   Not that
Shakespeare justifies usurpation; the crime will
surely work out its evil effects, but even the usurp-
ing Bolingbroke as compared with the sentimental
Richard—a royal poseur—may be regarded as a
"saviour of society".

30. Romantic tragedy as distinguished from

historical is represented by one work of early date. Romeo and Juliet stands alone as the lyrical tragedy of youth and love and death. The poet in Shakespeare, as we have said, somewhat embarrassed the dramatist in A Midsummer Night's Dream; the dramatist embarrassed the poet in the Rape of Lucrece. Here, in Romeo and Juliet, each aids the other, and the result .is a work harmonious and triumphant, in which song and speech become one or something rarer than either is born of the two. The play has no secondary action; our interest from first to last is centered upon the star-crossed lovers. Varying from his original, Shakespeare has accelerated the action of the story, so that the movement of the piece acquires a lyric swiftness and its passion a lyric intensity. Here for the first time on the English stage the terror of tragedy became beautiful. The spectator in the presence of untimely death and all the apparatus of the grave is not overwhelmed by gross horror, but sustained by the presence of beauty and the very chivalry of young love. There are tokens of immature workmanship in some portions of the play; inopportune conceits, overstrained ingenuities, over-florid diction; but we note such errors of style only to make us feel more vividly that in Romeo and Juliet we have still to do with the greatest of poets in his prime, when his adult art has not yet lost all traces of its adolescence. The mastery of his material appears as much in the humorous scenes as in the tragic. When we reflect that Mercutio and the Nurse are but subordinate figures we obtain some measure of the writer's affluence of creative power.

§ 31. But unlike "Juliet and her Romeo" there are lovers on whom all the stars shed favourable influence. In the Merchant of Venice Shakespeare makes amends for the piteousness of his tragedy by expending his finest art in making two human creatures happy. The play, as I take it, stands midway in the chronological sequence of the comedies between the earlier group of which I have spoken, and those later comedies which lie close, on either side, to the year 1600. In versification it has something in common with the Two Gentlemen of Verona, although its blank verse is far more vigorous and dramatic. In its strength and beauty of characterization it might take a place by the side of Much Ado about Nothing or Twelfth Night. The story of the caskets and the story of the pound of flesh are skilfully intertangled. The deeper interest of the play is over with the fourth act; but in the fifth we have a delightful epilogue; a counterfeit lovers'-quarrel must put an edge on the bliss of Bassanio and Portia. If any single thought presides over the double action of the comedy and reappears in a playful way in the fifth act it has reference to the moral force of bonds and promises and inherited obligations; but we must not, like the German critics, reduce the play, full as it is of life and its joys, to an abstraction. In none of the previous comedies can such breadth and strength of portraiture be found as here in the figure of Shylock. And even Juliet seems but a passionate child of the South when compared with the gracious lady of Belmont, so richly endowed with gifts of mind, so firm of will, so buoyant of temper, so noble in her

serious moods, so charming in her play, so great a
giver, yet so delicate in her art of giving.

§ 32. From comedy Shakespeare returned to history; from Italy he returned to England. In the
two parts of King Henry IV. and King Henry V.
he brought his series of English historical plays to
a close. The progress is great from King Richard
II. and King John. The dramatist has almost
escaped from the trammels of rhyme, and he has
learnt all the advantages of alternating verse with
prose. He knows how to ally the historical drama
with comedy now, not merely by an occasional
scene (like that of Jack Cade and his followers),
but by the presence of a great humorous personage.
The royal Bolingbroke, worn and saddened by the
weight of an usurper's crown, which yet he will not
resign till death discrown him, is at once a majestic and a pathetic figure. But he is almost over-
shadowed by the ample figure of King Falstaff on
his tavern throne. A French critic has placed Falstaff by the side of Panurge and Sancho as one of
the humorous trinity created by the Renaissance
imagination; but these seem compounded of simple
elements when compared with the rich amalgam of
comic qualities which make up Sir John. He dis-
appears of sad yet glorious necessity before we set
foot on the embattled plains of France. On the
stern field of Agincourt there is no place for a
champion so considerate on behalf of his own fat
carcass, and therefore Jack Falstaff must needs take
refuge from an ungrateful world in "Arthur's
bosom".

With the reign of Henry V. and the King's

laughing prophecy to his bride of a son "that shall
go to Constantinople and take the Turk by the
beard", Shakespeare almost touches the point from
which he had at first set out—the reign of Henry
VI. His portraits of English kings comprise that
of the pseudo-saint, a sorry plaything of circumstance, Henry VI.; the bold criminal, a warped
creature of dæmonic force, Richard III.; the royal
voluptuary and sentimentalist, Richard II.; the
usurper strong and prudent, Henry IV., master of
men and events so far as they can be controlled by
anxious care and firm volition; and finally Henry
V., in whom a frank goodness is at one with a
genius for empire and for battle. He is Shakespeare's ideal king of England, his ideal man of
action. Around him as around its centre the loyalty
of England, Scotland, Wales is organized. But
while thus presenting a series of historical portraits
Shakespeare also traces the logic of historical events,
and exhibits the law of moral retribution in process
from generation to generation, the abiding and
living influence of good and evil deeds. We read
in his plays, and with a remarkable degree of fulness and faithfulness, the ethics of English history,
deduced from the day of Bolingbroke's challenge of
Norfolk to the day when Richard and Elizabeth
entered on their heritage of loyalty and power.

These studies in English history gave breadth to
Shakespeare's view of the world; they saved him
from any danger there may have been of his narrowing as dramatist into an interpreter of the mere
romance of personal passion. And in shaping for
artistic purposes the substantial matter of history,

as he found it crudely presented in the chronicle of Holinshed, he gained strength and skill of hand; he could not here be fantastic; he could not permit himself to be misled by ingenuities and conceits; he must take his material as it was given to him, discover where it would yield and where it would resist, and so by prudent dealing mould it into dramatic form.

§ 33. It was probably while he was at work on the English historical plays, but at what precise date is undetermined, that Shakespeare made his recast of the old Taming of a Shrew, and wrote the admirably humorous Induction. We have good reason for believing that the Merry Wives of Windsor was an offshoot from King Henry IV. In the Shrew Shakespeare followed the lead of his dramatic predecessor; in the Merry Wives he worked by command, and, if we may trust the tradition, with unusual haste. The humour of both plays has something in common with that of the lower scenes of the later English histories. It would seem as if Shakespeare had carried over into comedy some of the roughness and realism of the comic part of the historical drama into which necessarily the romantic could not enter. Katherina is a very enjoyable whirlwind in petticoats; but we cannot place her by the side of Beatrice or Rosalind. English low life is presented in the miniature farce of Christopher Sly, old Sly's son of Burtonheath, pedlar, bear-herd, card-maker, and tinker; English middle-class life in the Fords and Pages of Windsor, with their laughing dames, that comely English maiden sweet Anne Page, her valiant lover young Master Slender, and

the learned justice Robert Shallow, of the county
of Gloucester, esquire. In King Henry V. the
Welshman plays his part and diverts the audience
with his courageous innocence and his "prave 'orts";
there is also some pretty fooling of the Princess
Katherine in her French-English. Here in the
Merry Wives the Welsh parson displays another
kind of valour from that of Fluellen with a like
valorous maiming of the King's English, and is
paired over against the French doctor, whose passion
is so cruelly cozened at the close. From plump
Jack Falstaff drinking water of Thames amid a
redundance of foul linen we piously avert our eyes.

The same buoyant temper which animates King
Henry V. and gives its breezy freshness to The
Merry Wives of Windsor is sustained in the romantic comedy of Much Ado About Nothing. Beatrice
and Benedick are perhaps a re-incarnation, and in
a finer stage of existence, of Rosaline and Biron in
the early comedy, which about this time Shakespeare revised and partly rewrote. How the gayest
spirits may be allied with good breeding Beatrice
will show us; she is not only witty, but also brave,
generous, and wise. And it is delightful to see how
a being so delightfully brilliant can be beguiled, not
to her destruction but to her own happiness, by the
blind leadings of her heart. If cleverness and infinite vivacity need their foil in pompous dulness,
we find that also in the play, for Dogberry and
goodman Verges climb to a height of sapient stu-
pidity and majestic ineptitude which borders on the
sublime.

Much Ado About Nothing was followed speedily

by As You Like It, and probably after no long interval by Twelfth Night. These three are the sunniest of Shakespeare's comedies. In the woods of Arden, indeed, the sunlight is tempered by green boughs; the good Duke lives in banishment, his daughter has had to fly from the usurper's court, and in Jaques we meet for the first time in Shakespeare's plays the satirist of humanity. But the Duke turns to sweetness his light adversity; Rosalind is not afflicted as she strolls through the woodland lawns which give Orlando shelter; Jaques, the dilettante satirist, is anything but a Timon, and in fact when he rails at mankind is only indulging an idle humour; and have we not Touchstone always at hand, moralist, courtier, critic, lover, poet, wit, to resolve wisdom's white ray into the prismatic colours of folly? In Twelfth Night all that is most mirthful and all that is most exquisite in the preceding comedies reappear with something of added mirth and grace. Malvolio would be too cruelly abused did not self-love make him his own chief deceiver, and self-importance protect him from some of the anguish of the discovery. The play has the gaiety and the good sense of the best comedies of Molière, with a tenderness and romantic beauty which lay beyond the art of the French dramatist.

§ 34. In the three comedies which follow these, and which bring the series for the present to a close— All's Well that Ends Well, Measure for Measure, and Troilus and Cressida[1]—a different spirit prevails. The strong-willed heroine of All's Well is a figure almost suited to tragedy; the play is a serious

---

[1] About the date of Troilus, however, there is some uncertainty.

study of the trials of heart of a woman who would strengthen and save a man above her in rank but far below her in character, one who through her aid alone can attain to moral worth and dignity. Parolles is almost too pitiful in his meanness to be a comic personage; the exposure of his cowardice is hardly worth the trouble it costs. The sunshine and frolic of Twelfth Night and As You Like It have disappeared; there is something forced in the laughter, or at least it is laughter which may quickly die away even if it should not turn to bitterness. Measure for Measure is more than grave; it would be dark were it not illuminated by the white light of Isabella's chastity. The vileness of a corrupt city is set before us with a painful realism. There are deep searchings and probings of the evil and deceitful heart of man. We are in the presence of death which is the fruit of sin; and life, the tender, florid life, shrinks back amazed and appalled from the grave and those vague vast regions to which it is the portal. But virtue stands embodied in Isabel, and providential forethought in the Duke, and therefore we are saved from despair. Measure for Measure is classed among the comedies, but it is a comedy which has gone astray and wandered uncertainly to the very borders of the realm of tragedy. Still more remote, however, from the true spirit of comedy is Troilus and Cressida. If Measure for Measure is dark, it is not bitter; the world which contains an Isabel is not a worthless or contemptible world. But in Troilus and Cressida life lies before us like an unweeded garden, " things rank and gross in nature possess it merely". I have elsewhere styled the play "the comedy of disillusion". We are introduced to heroic personages in order that we may be for ever cured of hero-worship. Troilus indeed is a gallant youth, but are we sure that he will remain as generous and ardent when he escapes from his boyish love-illusions? Ulysses is worldly wisdom embodied; but there is no ray of the heavenly to illuminate and consecrate this wisdom. The dog-like Thersites rails at all that we had supposed noble; we know that he is a dog, but is there not after all a vein of coarse plebeian truth in the railer's words? This is not a comedy gone astray, but a satire on human existence thrown into dramatic form.

§ 35. All the indications derived from Shakespeare's writings seem to point to the conclusion that there was a period of his life when, as Hallam says, "his heart was ill at ease and ill content with the world or his own conscience". We may take the year 1600 as a convenient date for marking the turn in Shakespeare's temper, which, however, was of course not a thing of an hour or a day. And it may be that in the obscure confessions of the Sonnets we find the key which unlocks the secrets of their writer's heart. That he passed about this time through a moral crisis seems certain. If we may trust the Sonnets, he had given away his affections to a friend who wronged him, and though in the end Shakespeare transcended his sense of injury, the pain and indignation left a deposit in his spirit. But, what was worse, he had himself chiefly to blame. He had yielded to the fascination of an unworthy love, and was betrayed by her who had played with all her art upon his passions, as a musician might play upon the strings of a lute; his pleasure, which at no time had been free from prickings of remorse, turned in the end to bitterness.   These experiences left him in no fit mood for the making of mirth; but if they darkened they deepened his knowledge of the human heart and its mysteries ot passion.   " The memory of hours misspent," goes on Hallam, soberest of critics, "the pang of affection misplaced or unrequited, the experience ot man's worser nature which intercourse with unworthy associates, by choice or circumstance, peculiarly teaches; these, as they sank down into the depths of his great mind, seem not only to have inspired into it the conception of Lear and Timon, but that of one primary character—the censurer of mankind."

M. James Darmesteter, as I have already mentioned, names the period during which Shakespeare produced his great tragedies and the darker comedies the Pessimist period.   I cannot accept the name. Shakespeare's nearest approach to what we call pessimism is not in Lear, nor even in Timon; it is in the comedy of Troilus and Cressida, which I believe preceded these.   As soon as Shakespeare set himself in the tragedies to a deeper study of the human heart and a more searching inquisition of evil, he made a fresh and higher discovery of human virtue.   By the side of the captive Lear stands Cordelia, whose spirit is calm with the strength of self-sacrificial love.   Edgar, the true justiciary, remains victor over the fallen body of Edmund.   If Timon despairs, it is because his heart was always weak, because he had lived among dreams and had never grasped the facts of life. No; Shakespeare was neither pessimist nor optimist; but a penetrating student of man's heart, who would deny neither the evil nor the good, neither the dark recesses of crime nor the illuminated heights of virtue.

§ 36. Two of the tragedies, the earliest in date, seem to me to stand somewhat apart from the rest —Hamlet and Julius Cæsar. I have called them "tragedies of reflection" as distinguished from the tempestuous tragedies of passion such as King Lear, Othello, and Timon. They may have preceded in the chronological order the joyless comedies of Measure for Measure and Troilus and Cressida. Neither Hamlet nor Brutus, who is the hero of the play of Julius Cæsar, is led on to destruction by his own passions; both are students, and we may say, philosophers; both are idealists; but Hamlet's ideals are laid waste, and the world grows sterile to his view; Brutus, on the contrary, lives and dies fortified by the moral doctrine which shuts him in from a true knowledge of the facts of existence and the characters of men; both Hamlet and Brutus are summoned to act on great occasions, and to both ideas are more real than deeds. Brutus indeed can act, and act with energy, but he misjudges men and events. Hamlet sees things more truly, but in him the continuous energy of the will is sapped, partly by excess of reflective power, partly by a barren despair about life. The errors of each arise, in a measure at least, from a certain nobility of character. They fall, but not dishonoured; we feel that they are spirits too erect or too delicate for the world of

fraud and violence in which it was their fate to move.
In King Henry V. Shakespeare had presented a
great man of action, a master of events. When we
have given him the meed of admiration which is his
due, we let him pass upon his glorious way. Hamlet,
who is no master of events, who executes his purpose desperately at last, and as it were by chance-
medley, whose life has effected so little that, com-
paring it with his great endowments, we may call
it a failure, interests us profoundly, and we return
again and again to gaze into the shadowy precincts
of his thought, and can never quite satisfy our
curiosity.

§ 37. Of the great tragedies of passion which
follow who can speak adequately? Perhaps the
least inadequate word ever said respecting them is
that fine extravagance of Goethe in Wilhelm Meister: "They are no fictions (*Gedichte*). You would
think while reading them, you stood before the un-
closed awful Books of Fate, while the whirlwind of
most impassioned life was howling through the
leaves, and tossing them fiercely to and fro." And
the speaker in Goethe's romance goes on to tell of
their tenderness as well as their strength, their calm
as well as their force. These terrible leaves of the
Book of Fate, which we name Macbeth, Othello,
Lear, Antony and Cleopatra, Coriolanus, Timon, are
all concerned with the breaches of the law wrought
by passion, the rending of the bonds of loyalty, of
wedlock, of filial duty, of love of country and love
of humanity; they represent man at odds with the
moral order of things; they exhibit evil in its incu-
bation and in its temporary triumph; passion in its

complexity of motion, its occult movements, its outbreak and violent fluctuations. But the effect left on the spirit of the reader or spectator of these plays is not one of disorder. The laws of human life are not shaken; the pillars of the divine order stand sure. Even though Cordelia lie strangled upon the lap of Lear we do not despair: "Upon such sacrifices the gods themselves throw incense."

§ 38. Othello (1604), founded on a tale in Cinthio's Hecatommithi, presents a striking contrast with Hamlet, which perhaps immediately preceded it in the chronological order. Here, instead of a student, the hero is a great soldier, a man framed for prompt and decisive action; instead of the reflective temperament of the North, we are shown in their terrible workings the torrid passions of the South; instead of wandering in vague mists and cloud we seem to encounter a simoom. The subtleties of Hamlet's intellect, the lingerings of Hamlet's will caused us to dread a grievous miscarriage of justice; it is the blind precipitancy of Othello's heart and hand which strikes us with terror. In the Moor there is somewhat of the grand simplicity of the barbarian, and he is taken in the toils of the craftiest and boldest brain in Italy. His love is a rapture of chivalry and fond protectiveness; his jealousy is no mean offspring of injured personal pride, but the anguish of despair for human purity and truth. Iago is Shakespeare's one absolute, irredeemable villain; irredeemable, because he has lost all faith in the existence of goodness, and because all passions are dead within him except those which gather about self. There is no weak point in his panoply

of disbelief and egoism; man and woman are
but tools in his hand which he uses, and despises
in the use. Two contrasted figures so superb and
so striking as Othello and Iago had never before
been set over against each other in tragedy; it is
still the ambition of great actors to present in turn
each of the two parts which demand such high and
such opposing accomplishments of art. Desdemona,
the very rose of purest passion, made to worship and
to be worshipped, is flung away like a noisome weed;
to slay her is as it were to slay love itself in its native
and original form. And yet we are made to feel
that love, not hatred, is the slayer. Desdemona dies
with the sacred falsehood of true love on her lips;
and Othello, in discovering her loyalty and exe-
cuting the doom upon himself, is restored to faith
and charity, if not to hope. It is the destroyer Iago
who really perishes as a withered branch from the
tree of humanity.

§ 39. In Othello the tragedy turns upon the rending of the bonds between husband and wife. In
King Lear (1605) the tragedy is that of violated
filial ties, and of a father saved—and scarcely saved—
from the despair, following upon unnatural cruelty,
by the redeeming passion of love in one daughter's
heart. The scale on which everything is presented
in this drama borders on the Titanic. The double
plot heightens and intensifies the effect. Gloucester's wrong and Gloucester's suffering are great, but
they fall well within the limits of humanity. The
passions of Lear almost break the bounds; there is
in them something vast and elemental; and Nature
herself, with her deluging streams, and fierce thrusts

of lightning, and reverberated thunders, seems to partake in and to reflect the chaos of the moral world. Where hatred, deceit, and egoism are outrageous, love is deep and still, a pure and quiet fount of blessing; Cordelia utters no passionate outcry, but all that is of virtuous power in the play organizes itself about her, or unconsciously takes part with her. She dies as the martyr of love; but when her father falls upon her body, and his strong, worn heart at last breaks through excess of strain, he is looking for that unuttered word of love upon her lips, the very expectation of which has saved him from despair and moral death. Cordelia dies, but love is not defeated.

§ 40. Macbeth (1606) probably followed next to King Lear. Our interest in this play is centred in the pair of wedded criminals; Duncan and Banquo and Macduff are figures of minor importance. Through an act of guilty ambition the bond—no longer a mere domestic bond—of loyalty between king and subject is severed; the culminating point in the action of the play is the murder of Duncan; the aspiring path to crime, and that dim blood-stained path which leads downward from crime to the abyss are traced in the earlier and in the later scenes. The essence of the tragedy lies not so much in the death of a virtuous king as in the parting of Macbeth from whatever possibilities for good lay within his nature. We watch him with an awful interest as we might watch one, beyond our reach to succour, who was slipping further and further down the edge of some ghastly precipice, clinging feebly for a time to grasses and shingle, and then fascinated by the horror of his descent, and plunging forward. Macbeth's wife is more finely organized than he; she weighs with steady hand the crown against the crime, and having willed the end, accepts with it the inevitable means. But, in assisting at the slaughter of Duncan, she has slain herself; her strength for crime is quickly exhausted; she is herself banished from life by those good laws of the world which she had violated. The witches are at once sublime and grotesque; they are not mere creatures of the brain like the dagger that appeared before the murderer's eyes; they are the incarnation of those evil powers which exist around us, if not in nature, assuredly in the world of human society, which are impotent against the man whose heart is set on righteousness, and lure to his ruin the man who pauses half-hearted between good and evil.

§ 41. Antony and Cleopatra (1607) and Coriolanus (1608) may be viewed as contrasted dramatic studies. In both plays a Roman is alienated from Rome; the bond between the citizen and his mother-country is in one case slowly dissolved, in the other it is violently strained and severed. The crime of Antony is that of a rich, pleasure-loving, voluptuous temperament; the crime of Coriolanus springs from overweening pride. Each is a great nature, magnificently endowed; and over each the influence of a woman—a mistress or a mother—dominates. Having painted in magic colours, as various as those of the shifting sea, the Eastern witch, Antony's " Serpent of Old Nilus", Shakespeare turned to carve, as it were in deathless marble, the figure of his Roman matron, a majestic caryatid upbearing the weight of the Roman household. Perhaps something of the great poet's political feeling may be discovered through his Coriolanus; he was certainly no democratic idealizer of the mob; if he acknowledged the good heart, he saw also the weak head of the people acting *en masse*, or swayed by the wily demagogue; but he had at the same time a clear perception of the vices of the patrician temper. We can well believe that neither an unbridled democracy nor an insolent aristocracy would have been altogether to Shakespeare's liking.

§ 42. The revolt against country in these two Roman plays passes into revolt against humanity in Timon of Athens. Only a portion of the play is from Shakespeare's hand; but that portion was written with full dramatic fervour. The misanthropy of Timon is the recoil from his own facile optimism; he had never known men as they are; his former careless generosity was far from true benevolence; his present hatred of the evil race of men is equally the passion of a dream. The creator of Timon, who put into his lips such eloquent invective against his kind, was himself no misanthrope. He had seen the evil and the good in the human heart; he would have the whole fact in his view and nothing but the fact; he desired, before all else, to see life whole; to be just of temper. And justice in a great mind necessarily results in gentleness when it has to deal with such creatures—so nobly endowed, so pathetically frail, so sublime, so ludicrous, so lovable—as man and woman.

§ 43. There are few transitions in literature more remarkable than that from Shakespeare's tragedies

of passion to the romantic plays, so grave and yet
so glad, of his closing years of authorship. It is
the transition from tempest, with its lightnings and
thunderings, to a wide and illuminated calm. The
writer of these exquisite plays, Cymbeline, The
Winter's Tale, The Tempest, has none of the light-
ness of heart which is the property of youth; he
knows the wrongs of life; he sees the errors of men;
but he seems to have found a resting-place of faith,
hope, charity. The dissonances are resolved into a
harmony; the spirit of the plays is one of large
benignity; they tell of the blessedness of the forgiveness of injuries; they show how broken bonds
between heart and heart may be repaired and re-
united; each play closes with a victory of love.
In Shakespeare's part of the drama of Pericles
several of the motives more fully developed in the
later plays are introduced; it is the story of loss
and recovery, through trial and sorrow, of a beloved
child. In Cymbeline husband and wife are parted
and for a while unjustly estranged, but only that
the joy of reunion may be more exquisite; while,
at the same moment, a royal father, after years of
sorrow for their disappearance, regains his long-lost
sons. In The Winter's Tale husband and wife are
again, and more cruelly, estranged; their infant
daughter is believed to have perished by a barbar-
ous death; but at the last all Hermione's wrongs
are forgiven in her silent embrace of Leontes, and
are recompensed, as far as recompense is possible,
by her possession of the child, now in all the bloom
of early womanhood, for whose loss she had so long
lamented. In The Tempest grievous wrong has

been wrought, and now the injured Duke of Milan has all the ill-doers in his power; but he has come to feel that "the rarer action is in virtue than in vengeance"; he uses his supernatural power to soften the hearts of the offenders, as far as that is possible with any of them, and then he wins back their love by his forgiveness. And here again the wisdom of those who attain through suffering is contrasted with the beautiful joy of youth which as yet has known no sorrow. Again there is a lost child restored—Ferdinand to his father the King of Naples; and again there is a rare environment of natural beauty, the strange sea and the island of enchantment, more wonderful, yet hardly more quickening to the spirit, than the stormy ocean and wide sea-coast of Pericles, the wild Welsh mountains of Cymbeline, the fields with primrose and daffodil of The Winter's Tale. The wrongs of life and how they may be transcended; trials of the affections; triumphs of fortitude and patience; magnanimous self-possession under suffering; love purified by grief, and in the end supreme over all; wisdom of the intellect at one with moral wisdom; the radiant joy of young and pure hearts:—these are the themes of Shakespeare's latest plays. Yet no moral is ever obtruded; the dramatist is intent only on duly presenting his characters and evolving their action. If the Shakespearian fragment Pericles be viewed as a kind of prologue to this group of plays, we may describe the Shakespearian fragment of King Henry VIII. as its epilogue. The same spirit in a great measure presides over this play, although, of course, its historical character causes that spirit to be the same with a difference. Queen Katherine is a Hermione of English history; she has a like dignity, a like magnanimous courage in adversity. It may be, as Dr. Garnett ingeniously argues, that The Tempest is Shakespeare's last complete play, and we gladly accept the idea of Campbell that the great enchanter of the imaginary world of the drama bade farewell to the stage in the person of his own Prospero; with him forswore his magic art, broke his staff of power, and sunk his book " deeper than did ever plummet sound ". If this be so, we may suppose that both The Tempest and its author's contribution to the pageant play of King Henry VIII. were written in his retirement at Stratford, and reflect the harmonious wisdom of his years of rural leisure.

§ 44. Looking back over the events of Shakespeare's life, and the series of his plays and poems, observing especially the Sonnets, where we may well believe the poet expresses his own feelings in his own person, we seem to see a man not naturally self-contained and self-possessed, but sensitive, eager, ardent, of strong passions, quick imagination, universal sympathy; at the same time a man with a central sanity of mind, and one for whom wisdom, knowledge, and self-control were constantly growing powers. So his material life, after certain errors natural to his temperament, was conducted to a prosperous issue; and his ideal life, passing through shine and shadow, touching all heights and depths of human experience, attained at the close a high table-land, where the light is clear and steadfast and the finest airs of heaven are breathed by man.

He sees human existence widely, calmly, with a temperate heart, with eyes purged and purified. And he sees perhaps not only the vision of life, but through it to deeper and larger things beyond. Shakespeare does not tell us what he saw when he looked beyond life with those calm experienced eyes. It was not his province to report such things to us as if he were God's spy. But assuredly he saw nothing which confused or clouded his soul; else he could not feel towards this our mortal life so purely, wisely, gently; else the great enchanter, this Prospero of ours, could not so tranquilly resign his magic robe and staff, dismiss his airy spirits, and piously accept the duties of mere manhood.[1]

III.

§ 45. Before passing on to speak of the growth of Shakespeare's fame a word may here be said of the doubtful plays of Shakespeare, or, as several of them may certainly be named, the pseudo-Shakespearian plays. Of these plays one early historical drama and one late romantic comedy have the best claim to contain work from Shakespeare's hand. The Raigne of King Edward the Third was entered on the Stationers' Register, Dec. 1, 1595, and was published in quarto in 1596. There is no external evidence to connect Shakespeare with the play, but Capell in his prolusions of 1760 called attention to a resemblance in style between this work and Shakespeare's "earlier performances", and to the

[1] In this paragraph I have appropriated a few sentences from an article of mine entitled Shakespeare's Wisdom of Life, which I have not reprinted since its first appearance.

fact that Holinshed's Chronicles and Painter's
Palace of Pleasure (both books having been certainly used by Shakespeare for the plots of plays)
supplied the fable.   Mr. Fleay believes that Edward III. was a play of Marlowe's which Shakespeare altered and revised.   The Shakespearian part
he holds to be from the entrance of King Edward
in the last scene of act i. to the end of act ii.
"For myself", writes Mr. Swinburne, who has made
a careful study of the play, "I am, and have always
been, perfectly satisfied with one single and simple
piece of evidence that Shakespeare had not a finger
in the concoction of King Edward III.   He was
the author of King Henry V."   If any man of
common judgment, Mr. Swinburne adds, can be
found to maintain the theory of Shakespeare's
possible partnership in the composition of the play,
"such a man will assuredly admit that the only
discernible or imaginable touches of his hand are
very slight, very few, and very early".   This last
statement expresses sufficiently nearly my own
opinion.   In the portion of King Edward III.
ascribed to Shakespeare by Mr. Fleay, the amorous
king makes an attempt upon the honour of the
Countess of Salisbury, which is met by a spirited
repulse.   With a reference to the Roman Lucrece
the king, now brought to his better mind, addresses
her:

> Arise, true English lady : whom our isle
> May better boast of, than e'er Roman might
> Of her, whose ransack'd treasury hath task'd
> The vain endeavours of so many pens.

It seems to me far from probable that the author

of the Rape of Lucrece is here alluding to his own poem.

§ 46. The romantic comedy of The Two Noble Kinsmen is of a much later date, and has certainly a far stronger claim to be considered as in part the work of Shakespeare. It was first printed in 1634, eleven years after our great dramatist's death, and on the title-page it bore his name as joint-author with Fletcher. Other external evidence than this there is none. The internal evidence yields a doubtful result. Several eminent critics—Coleridge, Hallam, Dyce, Sidney Walker, Mr. Swinburne, and others—have accepted the theory of Shakespeare's joint authorship, and schemes for the distribution of the acts and scenes between Fletcher and Shakespeare have been proposed.[1] But it is a remarkable fact that one of the most accomplished and careful students of the play, Professor Spalding, who in 1833 published an essay in which he endeavoured, with singular fineness of criticism, to draw the line between Shakespeare's handiwork and Fletcher's, declared in 1840 that his opinion was then "not so decided as it once was", and wrote in 1847 with increasing doubts that "the question of Shakespeare's share in this play is really insoluble". What happened in Spalding's case has probably happened with not a few persons, who at one time were assured that the hand of Shakespeare can be discerned in The Two Noble Kinsmen. The parts ascribed to him seem to grow less like his work in thought, feeling, and expression, as we, so to speak,

[1] Shakespeare's part: act i. (except part of sc. 2.); act ii. sc. 1; act. iii. sc. 1. 2; act. iv. sc. 3; act v. (except sc. 2).

live with them. The resemblance which at first impressed us so strongly seems to fade, or, if it remains, to be at most something superficial. At the present moment the drift of opinion is rather in favour of assigning the play to Fletcher and Massinger. The subject of The Two Noble Kinsmen is the story of Palamon and Arcite (told by Chaucer in his Knightes Tale), with which a wretched underplot, the work of Fletcher, is connected.

No intelligent reader of Locrine, Mucedorus, The London Prodigal, The Puritan, The Life and Death of Thomas Cromwell, The History of Sir John Oldcastle, Fair Em, The Birth of Merlin, can suppose that a single line was contributed to any one of these plays by Shakespeare. It is conceivable that touches from his hand may exist in A Yorkshire Tragedy, and even in Arden of Feversham. But the chance that this is actually the case is exceedingly small. We may therefore set down King Edward III. and The Two Noble Kinsmen as doubtful plays; the rest for which an idle claim has been made, should be named pseudo-Shakespearian.

IV.

§ 47. While Shakespeare lived his poems circulated widely and received high commendation; his plays were favourites with the people, and were also esteemed by the courtly patrons of the drama. It is probable that for some years after Shakespeare's death the plays of Fletcher were more popular upon the stage than those of any other writer. Ben Jonson was looked on as the great master of the scholarly or classical school of dramatic writing; he was, however, probably more praised by the judicious than enjoyed by the ordinary spectators of the theatre. Taste was deteriorating from Elizabethan days; the manlier temper of the drama was declining; and Shakespeare's plays soon came to be regarded as somewhat old-fashioned. Yet we know that several were enacted before Charles I., and were, as Sir Henry Herbert records in his Office Book, "well likte by the kinge". It was one of the virtues—not too numerous—of that loyal courtier and slight poet Sir John Suckling that he knew Shakespeare well; when his portrait was painted by Vandyke he was represented as holding in his left hand a folio on the edge of which is a paper bearing the name Shakespeare. The growth of Puritanism was of course unfavourable to the influence of a dramatic writer; yet Milton, the greatest poet of Puritanism, did honour in his earlier days to Shakespeare's memory in verses which tell of the profound impression made by the dramatist's "Delphic lines", and elsewhere celebrated him in contrast with Jonson, the poet of art and erudition, for "his native woodnotes wild". It was a grief to William Prynne, the author of Histrio-Mastix (1633), that "Shackspeer's Plaies are printed in the best Crowne paper, far better than most Bibles"; but that grief may have been allayed by knowledge of the fact that no "crowne paper" in folio form was used for this unworthy purpose during the period of the struggle against the bishops and the king.

In Restoration days, when the theatres were

G

reopened and possessed the new attraction of actresses in the female parts, there was something like a Shakespearian revival; but it was accompanied with the feeling that though Shakespeare was a glory of the elder English drama, he belonged to an age half-barbarous in comparison with one which had been refined by the growth of general culture and by influences derived from France. Killigrew's new theatre in Drury Lane opened with King Henry IV. The great actor Betterton appeared in several of Shakespeare's leading characters. The dramatist D'Avenant did honour to his memory. On Oct. 11, 1660, Mr. Samuel Pepys saw the " Moor of Venice " at the Cockpit, and on December 5 of the same year at the New Theatre " The Merry Wives of Windsor ". In later entries in his diary he mentions that he had been present at performances of Romeo and Juliet, "a play of itself the worst that ever I heard in my life"; A Midsummer Night's Dream, "the most insipid ridiculous play that ever I saw in my life"; Twelfth Night, "a silly play"; Macbeth, "a most excellent play for variety"; and to this last he returned again and again. The altered taste of the time made it seem necessary that Shakespeare's plays, in not a few instances, should be recast and modernized, a practice which was continued—and, as may readily be conceived, often with lamentable results—during the eighteenth century. The Tempest was altered by D'Avenant and Dryden, with added spectacle and song, new characters, and indecent dialogue. Antony and Cleopatra was improved upon by Sedley, Timon of Athens by Shadwell, Cymbeline by D'Urfey. Songs were written for Macbeth; Shylock was introduced at supper drinking a toast to his lady Money; Grumio of the Taming of the Shrew became a Scotchman. Tate made Edgar a lover of Cordelia, and gave the tragedy a happy denouement. Fortunately Hamlet escaped revision. With this old play even the polite Mr. Pepys was mightily pleased, and above all with Betterton in the leading character, "the best part, I believe, that ever man acted".

§ 48. Dryden venerated Shakespeare while he admitted (1663) that "others are now generally preferred before him". In "An Essay on Dramatic Poetry" (1668) he ventures to assert that Shakespeare "was the man who of all modern and perhaps ancient poets had the largest and most comprehensive soul"; but Dryden was not insensible to the fact that Shakespeare did not observe the laws of the drama as laid down by the critics whose authority was dominant in the Restoration period. His own All for Love, a play on the subject of Antony and Cleopatra, was written in blank verse, and he tells us that he aspired to imitate in his style "the divine Shakespeare". "The poet Æschylus", he says in his essay On the Grounds of Criticism in Tragedy (1679), "was held in the same veneration by the Athenians of after ages as Shakespeare is by us." This essay, which shows a more mature appreciation of Shakespeare's genius than appears in Dryden's earlier writings, is supposed by Dr. Johnson to have been occasioned by Thomas Rymer's Tragedies of the last Age considered and examined. In this and subsequent writings the

laborious compiler of the Foedera applies to Shakespeare the Aristotelian rules of tragedy, and finds
"in the neighing of a horse or the growling of a
mastiff . . . more humanity than many times in
the tragical flights of Shakespeare". Gildon and
Dennis replied to Rymer; and Dennis, who in his
better days was a far more intelligent critic than
Pope's satire would lead us to believe, wrote of
Shakespeare with sincere and ardent admiration.
"One may say of him," writes Dennis, "as they did
of Homer—that he had none to imitate, and is
himself inimitable. His imaginations were often
as just as they were bold and strong. He had a
natural discretion which never could have been
taught him, and his judgment was strong and
penetrating. He seems to have wanted nothing
but time and thought to have found out those rules
of which he appears so ignorant." When we reach
the age of Queen Anne we find the supremacy of
Shakespeare's genius generally acknowledged.

§ 49. The critical editions begin with that of
Nicholas Rowe, 1709. The demands of the seventeenth century had been satisfied by four editions in
folio, published respectively in 1623, 1632, 1663–64,
and 1685; if tried by the same test the popularity
of Jonson or Beaumont and Fletcher appears to
have been less considerable. Rowe did something
to purge the text of Shakespeare from its grosser
errors; he was himself a dramatic poet, and moreover, he was a man of good sense. His corrections
are not those of a collater of early editions or a
student of our elder literature, but such as would
occur to any cultivated and judicious reader. He

was the first to attempt to write a life of Shakespeare; it is a slender production, but has a value
as containing some traditions not elsewhere to be
found. Pope followed Rowe in 1725 with his
edition in six quarto volumes. "The minute mechanical examination which the enterprise required",
writes Pope's latest biographer, Mr. Courthope,
"was little suited to the broad and generalizing
genius of Pope's criticism, nor did he approach his
task in that spirit of sympathy with his author
which just editing requires. He altered some
expressions in the text because they seemed to him
vulgar, and others because the versification did not
conform to his ideas of harmony. Comparatively
little of his labour was spent in research, but some
of the conjectural emendations were happy, and
the Preface to the edition, written in his best
style—and his critical prose is always excellent—
deserves the high commendation that Johnson
bestows upon it." In this Preface indeed some
admirable thoughts are admirably expressed.
"Shakespeare is not so much an imitator, as an
instrument of nature." Can more be said in fewer
words? And on one of the controversies of his
own day he thus pronounces his opinion: "To
judge of Shakespeare by Aristotle's rules, is like
trying a man by the laws of one country who acted
under those of another". That Shakespeare was a
careless writer who never blotted a line is denied
by Pope, on the evidence of the varying text of the
quartos; nor was he an unlearned man, unless
"learning" means no more than "languages". The
Shakespearian drama in comparison with the more

finished and regular drama is like "an ancient majestick piece of Gothick architecture compared with a neat modern building. . . . It has much the greater variety, and much the nobler apartments; though we are often conducted to them by dark, odd, and uncouth passages. Nor does the whole fail to strike us with greater reverence, though many of the parts are childish, ill-placed, and unequal to its grandeur." Finer praise than this we could not expect from the Augustan age which delighted in Cato and the translation of Homer.

Pope's rival as an editor of Shakespeare, Louis Theobald, indebted to Pope, as he says, for some "flagrant civilities", if he was a duller man than his satirist of the Dunciad, was a far better Shakespearian scholar. His method of dealing with Shakespeare was to treat his text as that of a corrupt classic; and he claims to be the first to approach any modern author in this manner. He did some scholarly collation, and was often happy in his conjectural emendations. To him we owe "'a babbled o' green fields" in the account of Falstaff's death, and the reading, whether right or wrong, is one which alone might make an editor's reputation. His Shakespeare Restored, in which he exposes the errors of Pope, appeared in 1726; his edition of Shakespeare in 1733.

§ 50. The "Oxford Edition," in six quarto volumes, was published in 1744. The editor's name did not appear, but he was soon known to be Sir Thomas Hanmer. Collins celebrated the editor and his author in a poetical epistle, and the edition was

generally received with favour. A country gentleman of literary tastes, Hanmer had amused his
leisure hours, he tells us, with noting the obscurities
and absurdities introduced into the text, and according to the best of his judgment restoring the genuine
sense and purity of it. The emendations multiplied,
and "too partial friends" persuaded him to make
them public. Unfortunately he was not equipped
with the scholarship essential to editorial work.
"He did something to better", as Mr. Grant White
has justly said, "and somewhat more to injure the
text as Theobald left it." Three years later, in
1747, Warburton's edition, based on that of Pope,
appeared. In his preface he extravagantly over-
rates the value of Pope's work as an editor, and
attacks Theobald and Hanmer as having pirated
his own manuscript notes. The persuasions of
"dear Mr. Pope" induced Warburton to conde-
scend to a task so much beneath his high powers
as that of defending the true text of Shakespeare
from the wrongs done to it by dulness of apprehension and extravagance of conjecture. "Mr.
Pope was willing that *his* edition should be melted
down into mine, as it would, he said, afford him (so
great is the modesty of an ingenuous temper) a fit
opportunity of confessing his mistakes. In memory
of our friendship I have, therefore, made it our joint
edition." The modesty of an ingenuous temper
certainly was not a characteristic of Warburton.
His arrogance repels the reader, and when he goes
wrong, which happens very often, he does so with a
confidence amounting to effrontery. "Among the
commentators on Shakespeare", writes Hallam,

with no unjust severity, "Warburton, always striv-
ing to display his own acuteness and scorn of
others, deviates more than anyone else from the
meaning." Yet, having before him the work of
Theobald and Hanmer, whom he denounces, his
text is in some respects an improvement on that of
Pope. The edition drew forth severe criticism from
contemporary scholars — Zachary Grey, Heath,
Upton, and especially from Thomas Edwards in
his satirical Canons of Criticism. Dr. Johnson,
who honoured Warburton above his deserts, describes Edwards as ridiculing the editor's errors
with "airy petulance suitable enough to the levity
of the controversy"; while Grey attacks them "with
gloomy malignity, as if he were dragging to justice
an assassin or an incendiary".

§ 51. In the same year in which Warburton published his edition, 1747, David Garrick pronounced
at the opening of Drury Lane Theatre the lines in
which Johnson, with a fine extravagance, sounded
the praises of Shakespeare:—

> Each change of many-colour'd life he drew,
> Exhausted worlds, and then imagin'd new:
> Existence saw him spurn her bounded reign,
> And panting Time toil'd after him in vain.

Johnson's long-promised edition of Shakespeare
was completed in 1765. He consulted the earlier
texts to some extent, but was disqualified for the
task of minute collation by his defective eyesight.
As a conjectural emender he was not happy; he
tells us that as he practised conjecture more he
learned to trust it less, and after he had printed a

few plays resolved to insert none of his own readings in the text. His Preface is an admirable piece of criticism, robust and common-sense, though not illuminated by imagination, or very profound in its philosophical views. "This", he writes, "is the praise of Shakespeare, that his drama is the mirror of life; that he who has mazed his imagination in following the phantoms which other writers raise up before him, may here be cured of his delirious ecstasies by reading human sentiments in human language; by scenes from which a hermit may estimate the transactions of the world, and a confessor predict the progress of the passions." He defends Shakespeare from the censure incurred by his mingling comic with tragic scenes—here too the poet did no more than hold the mirror up to nature. Particularly noteworthy is Johnson's discussion of the doctrine of the unities of time and place; the spectators "are always in their senses, and know, from the first act to the last, that the stage is only a stage;" knowing which they can make time and place, as well as any other mode of being, obsequious to the imagination. After his manner as a critic Johnson sets his items of condemnation over against his items of praise; as a moralist he is offended by Shakespeare's sacrifice of virtue to convenience, his frequent violation of poetical justice; the plots are often loosely formed; the latter part of his plays especially is often neglected ; the poet has little regard to historical accuracy or local colour; his contests of wit are often marred by grossness ; in tragedy he is sometimes tumid and sometimes obscure; in narrative he

is often pompous and tedious ; his set speeches are
commonly cold and weak ; a quibble has a malig-
nant power over his mind, it is "the golden apple
for which he will always turn aside from his career,
or stoop from his elevation". Some of Johnson's
censures are just, but it is evident that from his
eighteenth century standpoint he never quite com-
prehended the spirit of Elizabethan poetry. His
knowledge of human nature renders some of his
analyses of Shakespeare's characters of peculiar
value ; his comment on the character of Polonius is
an example of passages which at once elucidate
the meaning of Shakespeare and exhibit the mind
of his critic.

In the late editions of Johnson (1773 onwards)
his work is connected with that of George Steevens.
Steevens had previously (1766) reprinted twenty of
Shakespeare's plays from the early quarto editions.
He was a man of industry, learning, and acute
intellect; somewhat wanting in reverence, somewhat wanting in modesty, and perhaps in that
literary honesty which goes with freedom from
vanity. His influence was a quickening one where
dulness and stagnation are dangers; but his ani-
mation was not of the best or purest kind. The
edition of Johnson and Steevens in fifteen volumes,
1793, often called "Steevens' own", is that which
shows his work at its best. In his editorial work he
remembered the earlier but not the closing words
of the motto found in Spenser: "Be bold, be bold,
be not too bold".

§ 52. The most laborious Shakespearian scholars
of the second half of the eighteenth century were

unquestionably Capell and Malone. "If the man would have come to me," said Dr. Johnson of Capell's Preface, "I would have endeavoured to endow his purposes with words; for as it is, he doth gabble monstrously." It is true that he expressed himself with awkwardness; but he had a true conception of the scholar's duty, and the preface of which Johnson speaks in this disparaging way has been justly described by competent authorities as the most valuable contribution to Shakespearian criticism that had yet appeared. All the quartos then accessible, and with them the folios, were collated by Capell. His text consequently is one of exceeding value, but unfortunately he did not assign the emendations which he adopted from other editors and critics to their individual authors. His edition is likely to disappoint a reader who comes to it for the first time, because it was issued without the valuable annotations and illustrations subsequently published in part in the year 1774, and after Capell's death in their entirety in three quarto volumes (1783) entitled Notes, Various Readings, and the School of Shakespeare. Valuable service was rendered by Capell in investigating the sources of Shakespeare's plots.

The work of Edmond Malone began with an Attempt to ascertain the Order in which the Plays attributed to Shakespeare were Written, which he handed over as a contribution to Steevens. This was followed in 1780 by a Supplement to the edition of 1778, containing the Poems, the doubtful plays of the Folio of 1664, and among his Prolegomena a study of the early history of the English

theatre. In 1790 he published his edition of the
Plays and Poems in ten volumes. His industry
was amazing; he was as honest as he was indus-
trious; and if he was not brilliant, like his rival
Steevens, he was free from the defects which sometimes accompany brilliancy in a critic. The debt
of all later Shakespeare students to Malone is in-
calculable. His studies and annotations are perhaps
best seen in the third "Variorum" edition of Shakespeare, 1821, edited by James Boswell from a copy
corrected by Malone. The earlier Variorum editions, called also the fifth and sixth editions of
Johnson and Steevens, appeared respectively in
1803 and 1813 under the editorship of Isaac Reed.

§ 53. Malone's erudition was well employed in the
exposure of the celebrated Ireland forgeries. The
father, Samuel Ireland, has suffered for the mis-
deeds of his son, Samuel William Henry Ireland,
who began his discreditable career by producing
for his father's delectation a forged document bear-
Shakespeare's signature. With the success of his
fraud the ambition of the young conveyancer's
apprentice took a higher flight. A large collection
of papers and relics obtained from an invisible old
gentleman came into the hands of the fortunate
youth. These included a love-letter to Anne Hathaway, a lock of Shakespeare's hair, his profession
of faith, and many other treasures. Those who
desired to believe in the authenticity of the papers
looked hard and saw what they wished to see. An
ancestor, with superfluous letters in his name,
William Henrye Irelaunde, had saved Shakespeare
from drowning in the Thames, and what less could

the grateful poet do than bequeath many papers
and books to his preserver for the delight of future
generations?   In due time a play of the great
dramatist came to light.   Vortigern was actually
presented at Drury Lane Theatre to a full house,
but no second night was possible.   Finally the
impostor came forward in 1796 with a confes-
sion; he was still under the age of twenty.   His
father suffered deeply from the disgrace, and died
in 1800.   William Henry Ireland survived until
1835.

§ 54. The critics of the eighteenth century—Grey,
Upton, Heath, Ritson, Monck Mason, and others,
were in the main textual critics of greater or less
ability.   Farmer's Essay on the Learning of Shakespeare (1767) deserves special mention; in this he
aims at proving that Shakespeare's knowledge of
the classics was derived from translations: "He
remembered", says Farmer, "perhaps enough of his
school-boy learning to put the *Hig, hag, hog*, into the
mouth of Sir Hugh Evans; and might pick up in
the writers of the time, or the course of his conversation, a familiar phrase or two of French or Italian:
but his *studies* were most demonstratively confined
to *nature* and *his own language*".   Another essay
of a different kind, Maurice Morgann's Dramatic
Character of Sir John Falstaff (1777), is a genial
piece of criticism, maintaining the thesis that Falstaff was no coward.   Charlotte Lennox, the friend
of Dr. Johnson, did something by her Shakespeare
Illustrated (1753–54) to render the materials from
which the dramatist formed his plots better known.
Another lady, Mrs. Montagu, ventured to come

forward with a defence of Shakespeare against the criticism of Voltaire. "When Shakespeare has got Mrs. Montagu for his defender", said Johnson, "he is in a poor state indeed." But Reynolds and Garrick were of a different opinion.

§ 55. A new school of criticism illuminated the study of Shakespeare in the early years of the present century. Coleridge in his lectures conceived art in general, and the dramatic art in particular, in a truer and higher way than any preceding writer. He was neither in bondage to Aristotle nor in revolt against him. He saw that the same spirit was expressing itself through Æschylus, Sophocles, and Shakespeare, though by methods which differed with all the differences of epochs and of races. He conceived Shakespeare's work as a whole; he observed the fruit as it hung in living beauty on the tree. And each play and poem he also conceived as a living whole. He studied its parts in their vital relation to one another; he did not murder to dissect. His analyses, or rather interpretations, of the characters of the *dramatis personæ*, are the outcome of a penetrative imagination; they are new creations, as it were, of the Shakespearian personages, transposed from poetry to criticism. He does not measure them by yard and line, but winds himself into their inner being and discovers the secret of their life. Unfortunately his criticisms have reached us, for the most part, in a fragmentary form; but often a sentence of Coleridge is, as it were, a lamp and a key, with the aid of which we can open and explore the mysteries of the dramatist's art for ourselves.

Hazlitt's light is not so pure, his leading is not so certain as Coleridge's; but he was ardent, and threw strong gleams upon certain parts of Shakespeare's work. Lamb, who touched nothing that he did not adorn, attempted no systematic body of criticism, but now with a loving phrase, now with a paradox, now with a quip or crank, now with a reminiscence from the stage, now with a brief analysis of character, he helps us to a truer understanding of Shakespeare. The Tales from Shakespeare by Lamb and his sister have served to introduce many young readers to the plays from which the narratives are derived. Among commentators of learning rather than genius in the first thirty years of this century Francis Douce was perhaps the most eminent. His Illustrations of Shakspeare and of Ancient Manners (1807) is a valuable storehouse of curious information. In 1817 appeared two quarto volumes entitled Shakespeare and his Times, by Nathan Drake, which in their day rendered useful service as a well-arranged compilation of facts, with agreeable comment by one who, though no original thinker, was a cultivated lover of literature.

§ 56. The most important editions of Shakespeare which have been issued since the Variorum of 1821 are those of Singer (1826),[1] Knight (1838–43), Collier (1841–44), Dyce (1857), Staunton (1857–60), Halliwell (Folio 1853–65), and the Cambridge edition (1863–66). Into the comparative merits of these it is not necessary to enter; but the learning

---

[1] The dates of the first editions are given; in several instances later editions much altered and improved have appeared.

and sound judgment of Dyce deserve a special acknowledgment, and no less the accuracy with which the Cambridge editors have done the work of collation, and the fulness with which they have recorded the conjectural readings of earlier editors and commentators. To these we must add the edition of the German Shakespeare scholar Delius (1854-61), and the American editions of R. Grant White (1857-65), Hudson (1851-56), and Rolfe (1884). Mr. Furness's Variorum Shakespeare (Philadelphia, 1871-92) sums up the work of all his predecessors with respect to the plays included in the volumes which have been issued; each volume is indeed a little library in itself; but work so laborious cannot be hastened, and as yet we have received only a few plays from this most judicious and learned editor.

The Shakespeare Society of England, in a series of volumes dating from 1841 to 1853, reprinted many rare and curious pieces of Elizabethan literature. In January, 1852, an eminent member of the society, J. Payne Collier, announced that three years previously he had obtained for a small sum from the bookseller Rodd a copy of the second Folio Shakespeare, containing many annotations—which he had not observed at first—in a hand of about the middle of the seventeenth century. This volume became famous as the Perkins Folio, deriving its name from the fact that it bore on the cover the inscription "Tho. Perkins his Booke". Collier supposed, or pretended to suppose, that the numerous corrections of the text, stage-directions, &c., were the work of an early owner of the volume, who through his connection with the theatre and attendance at performance of the plays had sources of trustworthy information as to the genuine text. Having previously given specimens of the "Old Corrector's" work, Collier towards the close of 1852 published a volume of "Notes and Emendations" which was alleged to include all the most important of the manuscript readings. When, in 1859, the Perkins Folio was submitted to the scrutiny of experts, the manuscript notes were declared to be modern forgeries. Pencil tracing was found to have guided the pen in its simulation of a seventeenth-century handwriting. Collier still maintained that the annotations were genuine, and controversy waxed warm. Competent authorities, however, could not be deluded, and unfortunately evidence had accumulated to confirm the impression that this really learned and ingenious scholar in not a few instances had yielded to the temptation to win for himself by fraudulent documents a spurious fame. It seemed to be the very wantonness of literary dishonesty.

The "New Shakspere Society", founded by Mr. Furnivall in 1874, applied itself with excellent results to the study of the peculiarities of Shakespeare's versification with a view to determining the chronology of the plays. It reprinted some of the early texts, and issued many interesting papers in illustration of Shakespeare. Indirectly it led to the most important service rendered in recent years to the student—the publication of facsimile reproductions of the early quartos. The first Folio had previously been made generally accessible by Booth's accurate reprint and Staunton's photo-zincographed facsimile. Among other aids to scholarship of recent or comparatively recent years the chief are the Concordance to the Plays, due to the loving industry of Mrs. Cowden Clarke (who with her husband, Charles Cowden Clarke, the friend of Keats, was also an editor of Shakespeare's works) and the Concordance to the Poems by the late Mrs. Furness; Schmidt's Shakespeare Lexicon, a monumental work; Hunter's Illustrations of the Life and Studies of Shakespeare (1845); W. Sidney Walker's Shakespeare's Versification (1854) and his Critical Examination of the Text of Shakespeare (1859); Professor Ward's solid and judicious History of English Dramatic Literature (1875); Mr. Fleay's Life and Work of Shakespeare (1886), in which the results of much research are united with ingenious, if not always trustworthy, conjecture; and Mr. Halliwell-Phillipps's Outlines of the Life of Shakespeare, a work which leaves little to be desired from a biographical point of view.

§ 57. At the same time what has been called the " æsthetic " study of Shakespeare advanced from the point at which it had been left by Coleridge. No critic, indeed, could penetrate more subtly to Shakespeare's meanings than Coleridge did; but his work was fragmentary, a series of admirable but disconnected notes. It remained to attempt the great task of interpreting Shakespeare's work in its totality. To this German students have at least led the way. Around the name of Shakespeare a vast library of German criticism has accumulated, and of this library a considerable portion is neither laboriously dull nor extravagantly theoretical. In Elizabethan days several of Shakespeare's plays were performed in Germany by English companies travelling on the Continent, and adaptations or imitations of them were produced by German playwrights. But our great poet's name was first mentioned in a German book in 1682; and even as late as 1740 Bodmer seems to have known our "Saspar" (so he prints the name) only as the author of A Midsummer Night's Dream. An attempt to translate Julius Cæsar into rhymed Alexandrines was made in 1741 by C. W. Von Borck, a Prussian minister of state, and seventeen years later an equally unhappy travesty of Romeo and Juliet was published at Basle. It was Lessing who first taught his countrymen to honour Shakespeare aright; opposing himself to the tyranny of French models on the stage, he maintained that judged even by the standards of antiquity Shakespeare, whom Voltaire had styled "le Corneille de Londres, grand fou d'ailleurs", was a higher dramatic poet than the Corneille of Paris. In 1762 appeared the first volume of Wieland's translation of twenty-two plays by Shakespeare, on which the later complete translation by Eschenburg (1775-77) was based. Garrick's acting of Hamlet was described to German readers by Lichenberg, and the manager of the Hamburg theatre, Schröder — a player of great eminence—put several of Shakespeare's tragedies upon the boards. Herder shared in that enthusiasm for our great dramatist which was extravagantly expressed by his younger contemporaries of the days of the Sturm und Drang. Goethe as a youth

prepared an oration in Shakespeare's honour; in
manhood he illuminated the tragedy of Hamlet by
his admirable criticism introduced into Wilhelm
Meister's Apprenticeship; in his elder years he declared that had he been born an Englishman, with
Shakespeare's masterpieces in their full might before
him, they would have overpowered his imagination,
and he would not have known where to turn to find
an opening for his creative instinct. Schiller adapted
the tragedy of Macbeth, Goethe that of Romeo and
Juliet, to the German stage. Two valuable gifts to
lovers of Shakespeare came from the Romantic
school—Schlegel's and Tieck's incomparable translation of the plays; and the criticism of Schlegel
on dramatic art and literature, first offered in 1808
to a Viennese audience in the form of lectures.   In
later years three important commentaries on the
complete works of Shakespeare have appeared in
Germany—that of Ulrici, which errs in German
fashion by reading into the dramas abstract ideas
of the critic's own theoretical mind; that of Gervinus, which is thoughtful and sensible, but somewhat laboriously moralizing; and the lectures of
Kreyssig, which seem to me to exhibit German
Shakespearian criticism at its best. The William
Shakespeare of Karl Elze is a work of solid erudition, and for the German student a mine of information. Since 1865 the German Shakespeare-Gesell-
schaft has published annually a volume of studies,
and among these the scholarly articles by Delius
deserve a special word of commendation.   In
Cotta's Morgenblatt of 1864, the year of the ter-
centenary of Shakespeare's birth, and in the early

numbers of 1865 appeared a series of " Shakespeare
Studies by a Realist" which attracted the attention
of a wide circle of readers; the articles were brilliant
in style, and it was refreshing in the midst of Teutonic enthusiasm and Teutonic earnestness to hear
the voice of a critical Mephistopheles who denied
the supremacy of the English dramatist. The
loyal adherents of Shakespeare directed each his
lance against this unknown and profane Paynim,
who before long was discovered to bear the name
of Rümelin. His attack rather stimulated than
checked the " Shakespeare-mania "; there is yet no
diminution of the seemingly inexhaustible stream
of German studies of our poet; it is still in Germany, as when Goethe wrote, " Shakespeare und
kein Ende".

§ 58. In France Voltaire called public attention
to the genius of Shakespeare, whom, however, he
represented as an intoxicated barbarian, "without
the smallest spark of good taste or the least knowledge of the rules". When in 1762 the French
Academy thanked Voltaire for his adaptation of
Julius Cæsar they confessed that they were unable
to obtain a copy of his English original. Ducis
adapted several of Shakespeare's plays—Romeo
and Juliet, Hamlet, Lear, Macbeth, and Othello—
to the French stage. Hamlet in Ducis' version lives
at the close of the play; with the story of the lovers
of Verona the adapter entangles that of Dante's
Ugolino. The versions, however, did much to make
Shakespeare better known. The first French translation of all Shakespeare's plays was that of Letour-
neur (1776-82). The tone of his author was in some

places altered to suit the taste of the age; but his enthusiasm for the English dramatist was evident. The ardent eulogy of Shakespeare by Diderot is characteristic of that great writer, who was in so many ways an imitator in criticism. Madame de Stael declared that while Shakespeare is the type of the English, or rather the Northern genius, the beauties of all countries and of all times may be found in his pages. In later years Guizot contributed to French literature a sober study of Shakespeare, and Victor Hugo a rhapsody of praise. Victor Hugo's son, François-Victor Hugo, executed an admirable translation of Shakespeare, and prefixed to each of the plays and poems an interesting essay. The best fruits of recent Shakespearian scholarship in France, besides Hugo's translation and that of M. Montégut, are the critical studies of M. Mézières, and M. Paul Stapfer whose work on Shakespeare and Classical Antiquity has been translated into English.[1]

§ 59. Among recent English studies Lady Martin's essays on Some of Shakespeare's Female Characters have an interest as the critical interpretations of one who was a distinguished interpreter of Shakespeare on the stage; they may be read with advantage in connection with the earlier criticism of Mrs. Jameson in her Characteristics of Women (1832). A series of thoughtful essays by W. W. Lloyd was contributed to the 1856 edition of Singer's Shakespeare and has since been separately published. Hudson's Shakespeare; his

[1] On Shakespeare in France see Lacroix's Histoire de l'Influence de Shakespeare sur le Théâtre français (1856).

Life, Art, and Characters, a thoughtful and sym-
pathetic piece of work, has achieved a deserved
popularity on both sides of the Atlantic. Mr.
Swinburne's A Study of Shakespeare (1880),
written with ardour and insight, characterizes the
three periods of the poet's development, the lyric
and fantastic period, the comic and historic, and
the tragic and romantic. Mr. Richard Moulton,
aiming at a popular illustration of the principles of
so-called "scientific criticism", has published some
excellent essays on "Shakespeare as a Dramatic
Artist" (1885). Two annotated editions of the
Sonnets have recently been published, the later,
that edited by Mr. Tyler, containing the results of
an ingenious endeavour to identify the persons of
the "Dark Lady" and "Mr. W. H." In number-
less editions the plays of Shakespeare have been
adapted to the purposes of education. Now, more
than at any previous period, our greatest poet, our
greatest Master of Life has a conspicuous part in
forming the mind of England.

§ 60. The interpretation of Shakespeare by
commentators and critics has been slow, laborious,
cumulative. There is another kind of interpretation which is vital, of immediate efficacy, and
directly addressed to a multitude roused for the
time to imaginative sympathy—the interpretation
of great actors; unfortunately this can be but coldly
and imperfectly transmitted to posterity, and hence
it must be ever begun anew. The greatest tragic
actor of Shakespeare's time was Richard Burbage.
It has been suggested that Hamlet was made "fat
and scant of breath" to suit the stout person of this

first Hamlet of the stage.[1] He was. especially identified in the popular imagination with the part of King Richard III., and his cry for "A horse! a horse!" lived on in the ears of a generation.[2]

§ 61. Of post-Restoration actors who interpreted Shakespeare the earliest and one of the most admirable was Thomas Betterton. For upwards of fifty years he held the stage, closing his dramatic career amid the unbounded enthusiasm of the spectators in 1710. He had the serious devotion to his art which is proper to a great artist; much personal dignity of life and manner; and his industry was amazing. He is said to have created a hundred and thirty new characters. His figure was not good; but his voice was of an enchanting quality; his countenance was expressive of passion as it were by a touch of nature, without strain or exaggeration. When as Prince of Denmark he encountered his father's spirit the actor's face turned "as white as his neckcloth". "When the Betterton-Brutus", says Colley Cibber, "was provoked in his dispute with Cassius, his spirit flew only to his eye; his steady look alone supplied that terror which he disdained an intemperance in his voice should rise to." His Othello and his Hamlet were in a special degree masterpieces. For the latter part it is said that he was instructed by D'Avenant in the traditions of the stage handed down from the days of Burbage and Taylor. The carping criticism of the one hostile contemporary, Anthony Aston, is

---

[1] "Faint and scant of breath" has been proposed, and the reading is adopted by Mr. Tree in his stage-version of the play.

[2] See the reference to Burbage as Richard in Bishop Corbet's *Iter Boreale.*

itself a testimony to the sound judgment of the great actor. "When he threw himself at Ophelia's feet, he appeared a little too grave for a young student just from the University of Wittenberg." Too grave!—as if Hamlet were in truth "your only jig-maker", and not rather among the saddest and gravest of mortal men. "His repartees", goes on Aston, "were more those of a philosopher than the sporting flashes of young Hamlet." "Sporting flashes" is good; yet who among Shakespeare's characters is a philosopher if Hamlet be not one? And we can well believe that if in this particular Betterton acted upon the hints received from D'Avenant, he was in fact embodying the conception of the part which Shakespeare himself may have expounded to his fellow players. "I never", says Cibber, "heard a line in tragedy come from Betterton, wherein my judgment, my ear, and my imagination were not fully satisfied, which, since his time, I cannot equally say of any one actor whatsoever." The triumphs of half a century did not overset the balance or mar the modesty of one whom Pepys described as "a very sober, serious man, and studious and humble, following of his studies". He had the happiness of companionship with a worthy wife, who was herself an artist of high ability. As Mistress Saunderson in Restoration days she played Ophelia to his Hamlet. Her Lady Macbeth was declared to excel even that of Mrs. Barry. She outlived her husband; but his loss was followed for her by the loss of reason.

§ 62. To Betterton's Hamlet, in the actor's early days, the ghost was played with admirable effect by his eminent successor on the stage, Barton Booth. Booth lacked, indeed, Betterton's regulated industry, but when roused he could toil with passionate force. It is perhaps most to be noted in Booth's honour, that while all the leading parts were in his hands, he would readily yield these to another—rarest of stage virtues—and himself show his fine powers in the minor personages of the drama. He played Laertes or Horatio as often as he played Hamlet. "Although his Othello was one of his grandest impersonations, he would take Cassio, in order to give an aspirant a chance of triumph in the Moor. In 'Macbeth' Booth played one night the hero of the piece; on another Banquo; and, on a third, the little part of Lennox. He was quite content that Cibber should play Wolsey, while he captivated the audience by enacting the King. His Henry was a mixture of frank humour, dignity, and sternness. Theophilus Cibber says enough to convince us that Booth, in the King, could be familiar without being vulgar, and that his anger was of the quality that excites terror. He pronounced the four words *Go thy ways, Kate*, with such a happy emphasis as to win admiration and applause: and 'when he said *Now to breakfast with what appetite you may*, his expression was rapid and vehement, and his look tremendous' ".[1]

§ 63. Robert Wilks, Irish by birth and education, and some years senior to Booth, excelled chiefly in comedy; but his Hamlet, and his Edgar in King Lear were remembered with admiration. He played the part of Buckingham in King Henry VIII. with

---

[1] Doran's Annals of the English Stage, ed. 1888, vol. i. pp. 413-414.

fire in the earlier scene and with pathetic dignity in
that which preceded his execution. His Prince
Hal is described by Davies as one of the most
perfect renderings of the theatre.   " At the Boar's
Head he was lively and frolicsome. In the recon-
ciliation with his father his penitence was ingenuous
and his promises of amendment were manly and
affecting. In the challenge with Hotspur his de-
fiance was bold, yet modest, and his triumph over
that impatient and imperious rebel was tempered
by generous regret." The stage Falstaff of the
same period, who in that part unquestionably surpassed all rivals, was James Quin. A third actor
of eminence, Charles Macklin,—like Wilks of Irish
origin—witnessed and shared in the stage history
of the eighteenth century during at least three of
its quarters. About 1725 he came to London; in
1789 with feeble frame and failing memory he
made his last appearance. The most important
incident in his career as a Shakespearian interpreter was undoubtedly his presentation of Shylock
in 1741. The Jew, during many years, had been
conceived basely as a low comic character, and
Shakespeare's play had been laid aside to make
room for Lord Lansdowne's unworthy alteration or
recast. Macklin revived the comedy in its original
beauty and grace; and he exhibited Shylock not
as a comic villain but as a character of tragic dignity. In 1772 he made an innovation in costume,
which may be noted as an indication that the town
was already touched by the romantic movement,
then in its earliest days; Macbeth, the thane of
Glamis, had been wont to appear on the stage in

the military costume of the day, with a tie-wig
and a suit of scarlet and gold; Macklin adopted
the national garb of Scotland, and saw that his
fellow-actors were also suitably dressed. It was as
Shylock that he attempted to act on his benefit
night when his age was either ninety or, as some
suppose, a hundred. "Who", he vaguely inquired,
"plays Shylock?" "Who? why you, sir; you are
dressed for it." " He put his hand to his forehead,
and in a pathetic tone deplored his waning memory;
and then went on the stage; spoke or tried to
speak two or three speeches; struggled with himself, made one or two fruitless efforts to get clear,
and then paused, collected his thoughts, and, in a
few mournful words, acknowledged his inability,
asked pardon, and under the farewell applause of
the house, was led off the stage for ever." [1]

§ 64. The year 1741, memorable for Macklin's
restoration of the true Shylock, was yet more
memorable through the presentation at the little
theatre in Ayliffe Street, Goodman's Fields, of
King Richard III. by "a gentleman", as the bills
announced, "who never appeared on any stage".
It was not strictly true that David Garrick (then
twenty-six years of age) had not previously acted in
public. He had appeared with applause at Ipswich,
but before October, 1741, he had not faced the
London public. The spectators were astonished
and delighted by the revelation of a new and
wonderful power. Every turn of passion, intellectual pride, humour, irony, rage, despair, were
rendered with infallible effect; within a single part

---

[1] Doran: Annals of the English Stage, vol. iii. pp. 74, 75.

a wide range of versatility was demonstrated.
Soon the more fashionable theatres were emptied,
and trains of carriages and crowds on foot
gathered to Goodman's Fields. Here was indeed
the true successor of Betterton. His audience, says
a historian of the stage, were especially impressed
by Garrick's "nature"—that is to say, his truth to
life. A mechanical method of delivery had since
the days of Betterton got possession of the theatre;
Garrick's elocution was the natural elocution of
passion, refined by art. "The chuckling exultation
of his 'So much for Buckingham!' was long a tradition on the stage. . . . The rage and rapidity with
which he delivered

'Cold friends to me! What do they in the North,
When they should serve their sovereign in the West?

made a wonderful impression on the audience.
Hogarth has shown us how he looked when start-
ing from his dream; and critics tell us that his cry
of 'Give me another horse!' was the cry of a gallant,
fearless man; but that it fell into one of distress as
he said 'Bind up my wounds', while the 'Have
mercy, Heaven!' was moaned piteously on bended
knee." "Garrick", said Quin, "is a new religion;
the people follow him as another Whitfield, but
they will soon return to church again." They did
not, however, prove as willing as Quin supposed to
return from the religion of genuine nature to the
church of stage convention.

Next year, 1742, Garrick quitted Goodman's
Fields for Drury Lane, and while continuing his
Richard III. he added to his repertory the difficult

part of King Lear. The distraction and despair of
the afflicted king were studied from life; a gentleman of Garrick's acquaintance had been through
a melancholy accident the cause of his daughter's
death; his reason forsook him, and it was his habit
to go frequently to the window from which he had
allowed the child to fall, and there to re-enact his
last caresses, his agony, and his despair. From
suggestions derived thence and heightened by his
own genius, Garrick created his heart-breaking exposition of Lear's anguish as he hangs over the
body of Cordelia. "In that exquisite performance,"
writes Galt, "which touched the heart of the spectators with a sympathy more like grief than only
sympathy, he had no sudden starts nor violent ges-
ticulations; his movements were slow and feeble,
misery was in his look, he fearfully moved his head,
his eyes were fixed and glittering without specu-
lation; when he turned to those around him he
paused, seemed to be summoning remembrance,
and in every sad and demented feature expressed
a total alienation of mind."[1] Thirteen years later
Garrick gave his rendering of Lear as it were in
rivalry with the handsome young Irish actor,
Spranger Barry. An epigram of the day puts in
brief the judgment of the wits respecting this con-
test:—

> The town has found out diff'rent ways,
>   To praise the different Lears;
> To Barry they gave loud huzzas!
>   To Garrick—only tears.

---

[1] Lives of the Players, vol. i. p. 257. In this passage Galt is "con-
veying" somewhat liberally from Murphy's Life of Garrick.

On an earlier occasion the rivalry between the same two actors—the one appearing at Drury Lane, the other at Covent Garden—was in the character of Romeo. In the garden scenes Barry excelled; Garrick surpassed him in the meetings of Romeo with the Friar and the Apothecary. "Had I been Juliet to Garrick's Romeo," said a lady who witnessed both performances, "so ardent and impassioned was he, I should have expected that he would have *come up* to me in the balcony; but had I been Juliet to Barry's Romeo, so tender, so eloquent, and so seductive was he, I should certainly have *gone down* to him." Garrick's Juliet, Miss Bellamy, was, however, more ardent in her passion than Mrs. Cibber, who played with his rival. In Othello, where Barry succeeded, Garrick may be said to have failed; but his Hamlet and his Macbeth more than made amends. Through Hamlet's emotion in presence of the ghost, the supernatural seemed for the spectators to become a reality. His colour left his cheeks; his voice became low and interrupted; he stood an image of awe, pity, reverence, and horror.[1] Garrick as Macbeth was praised more for "nature" than for heroism. In the dagger scene he was especially impressive; his rendering is said to have differed as widely from the "majestic solemnity" of John Kemble as from the "restless ecstasy" of Quin.

§ 65. In 1776 Garrick took his leave of the stage. Five nights before that farewell he played his first

---

[1] The most interesting account of Garrick as Hamlet is that written by the German Lichtenberg, who is perhaps best remembered in connection with the study of Hogarth in Germany. See also in Tom Jones, book xvi. chap. v., the visit of Partridge to the playhouse

great part—that of Richard III.—to the Lady Anne of Sarah Siddons. Her first appearance at Drury Lane had been six months previously, when, on December 29, 1775, her Portia was announced as to be taken "by a young lady". She was now in her twenty-first year, and had been married since November, 1773. She belonged from her birth to the stage; both Roger Kemble, her father, and his wife were strolling players. She made her first appearance at so early an age that the audience were roused to indignant pity, which was appeased only by her happy recitation of the fable "The Boys and Frogs". Success came to her first in Bath, and when in 1782 she passed from Bath to London, the peals of applause which greeted her were such as probably no actress had hitherto won. In comedy, indeed, she achieved no triumph; her genius was essentially of a tragic cast. Her Constance, Desdemona, Volumnia, Cordelia were great and original impersonations. Perhaps her highest achievements were in the part of the royal criminal, Lady Macbeth, and that of the royal saint, Queen Katharine. "Mrs. Siddons", writes Doran, "imagined Lady Macbeth, the heroine of the most tragic of tragedies, to be a delicate blonde, who ruled by her intellect, and subdued by her beauty, but with whom no one feeling of common general nature was congenial; a woman prompt for wickedness, but swiftly possessed by remorse; one who is horror-stricken for herself and for the precious husband, who, more robust and less sensitive, plunges deeper into crime, and is less moved by any sense of compassion or sorrow." Galt speaks from his

personal recollection of the deep impression produced by the "low deep accent of apprehension,
or of conscious conspiracy which she sustained
throughout, especially as it influenced the utterance
of her Medean invocation to the

Spirits that tend on mortal thought,

and still more in the subsequent scene, where she
chastises with her valour the hesitation of Macbeth".
The sleep-walking scene was, he adds, so tremendous that whether literal in its truth to nature or
not, with such a character, gnawed with the Pro-
methean agonies of crime, it ought to have been
natural. Her Queen Katharine is described by the
same writer as only inferior to the sublimity of
Lady Macbeth, yet hardly comparable with that
part as being of so different a kind: "The manner
in which she retired from the trial scene was equal
to her grandeur at the banquet in *Macbeth*, and the
sensibility with which she uttered 'God help me!'
as she quitted the room, was perhaps the most
exquisitely just expression of grief and feeling ever
uttered in representation. I should, however, only
tire in prolonging the description of her dignity and
sensibility. Her excellence in these two great and
rare qualities constituted the main ingredient of her
amazing sorcery." Mrs. Siddons retired from the
stage in June 1812, closing her great career in the
part of Lady Macbeth. Her rare appearances on
subsequent occasions ceased in 1819. The greatest
of tragic actresses was a true and admirable woman
in her domestic life; she had toiled for her children
and endured with courageous resignation the sorrow

I

of surviving all of them but one.   When her death took place on June 8, 1831, it was felt that a light and glory of England had been extinguished.

§ 66. Sarah Siddons' brother, Charles Kemble, became, by force of some native talent and much careful study, a graceful and refined actor.   His Cassio, Faulconbridge, Macduff, Edgar, were each the best rendering of the part in his time.   But his fame was obscured by the greater glory of his elder brother, John Philip Kemble.   After some training at provincial theatres he appeared in 1783 at Drury Lane as Hamlet, and it was quickly felt that a new and distinguished actor had come upon the boards. Two years later he played Othello to his sister's Desdemona, and Macbeth to his sister's Lady Macbeth.   His Lear, played in 1788 to his sister's Cordelia, was one of his most admirable performances. But it was in his Roman parts that John Kemble, with his noble figure and stately manner, showed to most advantage; in particular he identified himself with Shakespeare's Coriolanus.   " Had he only acted in that character," writes a critic who was not insensible to the weaknesses of Kemble's stately mannerism, "he would have been deemed the very greatest male actor ever seen; it was in all points of conception, look, and utterance equal to the Lady Macbeth of Mrs. Siddons.   In no other part whatever did he, or could he, attain equal eminence." John Kemble had received a liberal education at Douay, and he possessed in addition to his genius as an actor, something of a scholar's feeling for precision of detail in the representation of a play and in the arrangements of the stage.   He had the disadvantage of a weak voice; but his clear and measured elocution added a beauty to poetry if it were eloquent and rhetorical. He often failed to interpret the quick and various turns of passion, but where a steadfast strength of feeling or pathos, allied to dignity, demanded expression, he was in a high degree impressive.

§ 67. The Kemble dynasty, if it did not fall, tottered before the irresistible onset of Edmund Kean's genius. For sheer force of that which can only be conferred by divine gift—genius in the exposition of passion—Kean probably ranks highest among all actors of our English race. Each of his greater renderings of Shakespeare was an inspired commentary on the inmost spirit of the play. His imaginative energy of feeling penetrated to the heart of the mystery of each character which he assumed, or, to speak more correctiy, which for the time he became. Even as we read the poor records and analyses of his presentations of Shakespearian characters, they are a light and a guide to criticism.

Edmund Kean was born in 1787, the child of a worthless mother who gave him only coldness, neglect, or cruelty. At three years old he was the Cupid of a ballet. All his earlier years were a ceaseless struggle against poverty, disappointment, almost despair; and yet there was that within him which made total despair impossible. In 1813 hope lit up his prospects; but bitterness was even then mingled with his joy. Dr. Drury, a member of the Drury Lane Committee, discovered his extraordinary powers, while he was playing as a stroller at Dorchester; an engagement was promised him, but before he could leave Dorchester his first son, Howard, with whom his heart was bound up, had died. The 26th of February, 1814, was the most memorable day in the life of Edmund Kean, and one of the most memorable in the history of the English stage. At length his opportunity had come; on that evening he appeared at Drury Lane in the character of Shylock. As he trudged on foot through snow and fog to the theatre, " I wish", he exclaimed, " I was going to be shot!" When the curtain fell it was known to those who could discern that the greatest exponent of human passion ever seen upon the English stage had appeared. He hurried back to his poor lodgings; " Mary," he cried to his wife, " you shall ride in your carriage"; and to his infant Charles, " You shall go to Eton"; and then his face saddened as the words broke from him, " If Howard had but lived to see it!"

§ 68. To follow Kean through his successive triumphs is impossible in such a brief sketch as the present. His King Richard III. was a masterpiece even more extraordinary than his Shylock. The disadvantages of his small figure and sometimes harsh voice were entirely overcome or were forgotten; his pale face was illuminated with the inspiration of his mind. " Joyous and sarcastic in the opening soliloquy; devilish as he passed his bright sword through the still breathing body of Lancaster; audaciously hypocritical, and almost too exulting in the wooing of Lady Anne; cruelly kind to the young Princes, his eye smiling while his foot seemed restless to crush the two spiders that so vexed his heart; in representing all this there was an origin-

ality and a nature which were entirely new to the
delighted audience. Then they seemed to behold
altogether a new man revealed to them, in the first
words uttered by him from the throne,—' Stand all
apart!' from which period to the last struggle with
Richmond there was an uninterrupted succession
of beauties. . . . The triumph was accumulative,
and it was crowned by the tent scene, the battle,
and the death. . . . In the faint yet deadly-meant
passes which he made with his swordless arm after
he had received his death-blow, there was the conception of a great artist ; and there died with him
a malignity which mortal man had never before so
terribly portrayed."[1]

§ 69. Hamlet and Othello succeeded King Richard III., and in neither did any diminution of power
appear. The passionate tenderness and the passionate fierceness of Othello were indeed rendered
as they had never been rendered before.[2] Macbeth,
Romeo, Richard II., Timon showed under various
aspects the same astonishing genius in the interpretation of passion. In 1820 Kean enacted for the first
time the part of King Lear. He had studied and
rehearsed with ardour; on one occasion he played
scene after scene before the pier-glass from midnight
to noonday; in order to qualify himself for the representation of the distracted king, he constantly
visited the St. Luke's and Bethlehem hospitals. He
determined in 1823 to discard the mawkish version
of the play by Nahum Tate, and to retain the tragic

---

[1] Doran: Annals, vol. iii. pp. 380, 381.
[2] See a remarkable criticism of Kean's Othello in Letters on England by Victoire Count de Soligny, *i.e.* P. G. Patmore, vol. ii. pp. 96–
118.

close as imagined by Shakespeare. "There", he
said to his wife, pointing to the last scene of Lear,
"is the sacred page I am yet to expound." When
his Othello was alleged to be the most sublime and
impressive creation of his genius, he replied, "The
London audience have no notion of what I can do
until they see me over the dead body of Cordelia".
And so in truth it was; a competent judge who had
witnessed Garrick's performance of the part pronounced it inferior to that of Kean. "Who", asks
his biographer, Hawkins, "that once heard can ever
forget the terrors of that terrific curse, where, in the
wild storm of his conflicting passion, he threw himself on his knees, 'lifted up his arms, like withered
stumps, threw his head quite back, and, in that
position, as if severed from all that held him to
society, breathed a heart-struck prayer, like the
figure of a man obtruncated'?" An American writer,
Dana, conveys some impression of Kean's rendering
of the insanity of Lear: "His eye, when his senses
are first forsaking him, giving a questioning look at
what he saw, as if all before him was undergoing a
strange and bewildering change which confused his
brain—the wandering, lost motions of his hands which
seemed feeling for something familiar to them, on
which they might take hold and be assured of a safe
reality—the under monotone of his voice, as if he
was questioning his own being and all which surrounded him—the continuous, but slight oscillating
motion of the body,—all expressed, with fearful
truth, the dreamy state of a mind fast unsettling,
and making vain and weak efforts to find its way
back to its wonted reason. There was a childish,

feeble gladness in the eye, and a half-piteous smile about the mouth at times, which one could scarce look upon without shedding tears. As the derangement increased upon him, his eye lost its notice of what surrounded him, wandering over everything as if he saw it not, and fastening upon the creatures of his crazed brain. The helpless and delighted fondness with which he clings to Edgar as an insane brother is another instance of the justness of Mr. Kean's conceptions. Nor does he lose the air of insanity even in the fine moralizing parts, and where he inveighs against the corruptions of the world. There is a madness even in his reason."

Edmund Kean, now a broken and feeble man, was playing his great part of Othello to the Iago of his son Charles on March 25, 1833, when the end came. Having spoken with the old beauty of feeling and expression Othello's farewell to the occupation of his life, he could not proceed with the next speech; he fell upon his son's shoulder, whispering, "I am dying—speak to them for me". He was borne off the stage, and after a lingering period of weakness, died on May 15 of that year.

§ 70. When the stage lost Kean there was no one who could fill his place; an actor of his kind does not arise twice in a century. But Macready was in the plenitude of such power as he possessed, and he carried on with much dignity, culture, and intellectual skill, the tradition of the stately school of Kemble, qualified by something of Kean's pathetic power. His first appearance at Covent Garden Theatre was in 1816; in 1819 he produced considerable effect in the part of Richard III. In 1837 he became lessee and manager of Covent Garden, and his managership was honourably distinguished by a series of Shakespearian revivals which, if not a pecuniary success, were certainly full of interest from the artistic point of view. Macready with his cultivated taste did not aim at merely starring it with one great part which should stand out from a dead level of general mediocrity. He endeavoured to make the rendering of the entire play harmonious. In 1851 this excellent actor and most estimable man retired from the stage. He had helped to interpret Shakespeare by his own graceful and intellectual renderings of individual parts, and still more by that harmony in presenting the whole after which he studiously sought.

At this point—the mid-point of the present century — this brief sketch of Shakespearian stage-history may fitly close. Much has been omitted; Mrs. Pritchard, Mrs. Cibber, Mrs. Jordan, and, in comparatively recent years, Henderson, Cooke, Charles Kean, and many another actor, might each, in a fuller record, fitly claim a notice. Not a little has been done in illustration of Shakespeare since 1851; new and admirable achievements have glorified our stage; great names have sprung into the light of fame. But it is well that criticism should pause at a point somewhat remote from the present moment. The year of the first Great Exhibition will serve sufficiently well for a resting-place.

APPENDIX.

DEDICATION PREFIXED TO THE FOLIO
OF 1623.

To the most noble and incomparable pair of brethren,
William Earl of Pembroke, &c., Lord Chamberlain to the King's
most excellent majesty,
and
Philip Earl of Montgomery, &c., Gentleman of his majesty's bed-
chamber;
Both Knights of the most noble order of the Garter, and our singular
good lords.

RIGHT HONOURABLE,

Whilst we study to be thankful in our particular
for the many favours we have received from your L.L., we
are fallen upon the ill fortune, to mingle two the most diverse
things that can be, fear and rashness,—rashness in the enterprise, and fear of the success. For when we value the places
your H.H. sustain, we cannot but know their dignity greater
than to descend to the reading of these trifles; and while we
name them trifles, we have deprived ourselves of the defence
of our dedication. But since your L.L. have been pleased to
think these trifles something heretofore, and have prosecuted
both them and their author living with so much favour, we
hope that (they outliving him, and he not having the fate,
common with some, to be executor to his own writings) you
will use the like indulgence toward them you have done unto
their parent. There is a great difference whether any book
choose his patrons, or find them: this hath done both. For
so much were your L.L. likings of the several parts when
they were acted, as before they were published, the volume
asked to be yours. We have but collected them, and done
an office to the dead, to procure his orphans guardians;
without ambition either of self-profit or fame; only to keep
the memory of so worthy a friend and fellow alive as was our

Shakespeare, by humble offer of his plays to your most noble patronage. Wherein, as we have justly observed no man to come near your L.L. but with a kind of religious address, it hath been the height of our care, who are the presenters, to make the present worthy of your H.H. by the perfection. But there we must also crave our abilities to be considered, my lords. We cannot go beyond our own powers. Country hands reach forth milk, cream, fruits, or what they have; and many nations, we have heard, that had not gums and incense, obtained their requests with a leavened cake. It was no fault to approach their gods by what means they could: and the most, though meanest, of things are made more precious when they are dedicated to temples. In that name, therefore, we most humbly consecrate to your H.H. these remains of your servant Shakespeare, that what delight is in them may be ever your L.L., the reputation his, and the faults ours, if any be committed by a pair so careful to show their gratitude both to the living and the dead as is

Your Lordships' most bounden,

JOHN HEMINGE,
HENRY CONDELL.

———————

ADDRESS PREFIXED TO THE FOLIO OF 1623.

To the great variety of readers.

From the most able to him that can but spell: there you are numbered. We had rather you were weighed: especially when the fate of all books depends upon your capacities; and not of your heads alone, but of your purses. Well, it is now public; and you will stand for your privileges, we know,—to read and censure. Do so, but buy it first: that doth best commend a book, the stationer says. Then how odd soever your brains be or your wisdoms, make your license the same, and spare not. Judge your six-pen'orth, your shillings-worth, your five-shillings-worth at a time, or higher, so you rise to the just rates, and welcome. But, whatever you do, buy.

Censure will not drive a trade, or make the jack go. And though you be a magistrate of wit, and sit on the stage at Black-friars or the Cock-pit, to arraign plays daily, know, these plays have had their trial already, and stood out all appeals, and do now come forth quitted rather by a decree of court than any purchased letters of commendation.

It had been a thing, we confess, worthy to have been wished, that the author himself had lived to have set forth and overseen his own writings. But, since it hath been ordained otherwise, and he by death departed from that right, we pray you do not envy his friends the office of their care and pain, to have collected and published them; and so to have published them as where before you were abused with divers stolen and surreptitious copies, maimed and deformed by the frauds and stealths of injurious impostors that exposed them, even those are now offered to your view cured and perfect of their limbs, and all the rest absolute in their numbers as he conceived them; who, as he was a happy imitator of nature, was a most gentle expresser of it: his mind and hand went together; and what he thought, he uttered with that easiness, that we have scarce received from him a blot in his papers. But it is not our province, who only gather his works and give them you, to praise him. It is yours that read him: and there we hope, to your divers capacities, you will find enough both to draw and hold you; for his wit can no more lie hid than it could be lost. Read him, therefore; and again and again: and if then you do not like him, surely you are in some manifest danger not to understand him. And so we leave you to other of his friends, whom if you need, can be your guides: if you need them not, you can lead yourselves and others. And such readers we wish him.

JOHN HEMINGE,
HENRY CONDELL.

COMMENDATORY VERSES FROM THOSE PREFIXED TO THE FOLIO OF 1623.

To the memory of my beloved, the author, Master William Shake-
speare, and what he hath left us.

To draw no envy, Shakespeare, on thy name,
Am I thus ample to thy book and fame;
While I confess thy writings to be such
As neither man nor Muse can praise too much:
'Tis true, and all men's suffrage: but these ways
Were not the paths I meant unto thy praise;
For seeliest ignorance on these may light,
Which, when it sounds at best, but echoes right;
Or blind affection, which doth ne'er advance
The truth, but gropes, and urgeth all by chance;
Or crafty malice might pretend this praise,
And think to ruin where it seem'd to raise:
.   .   .   .
But thou art proof against them; and, indeed,
Above th' ill fortune of them or the need.
I, therefore, will begin.   Soul of the age,
Th' applause, delight, the wonder of our stage,
My Shakespeare, rise !   I will not lodge thee by
Chaucer or Spenser, or bid Beaumont lie
A little further, to make thee a room:
Thou art a monument without a tomb,
And art alive still, while thy book doth live,
And we have wits to read, and praise to give.
That I not mix thee so, my brain excuses,—
I mean, with great but disproportioned Muses;
For if I thought my judgment were of years,
I should commit thee surely with thy peers,
And tell how far thou didst our Lyly outshine,
Or sporting Kyd, or Marlowe's mighty line:
And though thou hadst small Latin and less Greek,
From thence to honour thee I would not seek
For names; but call forth thundering Æschylus,
Euripides, and Sophocles to us,

Pacuvius, Accius, him of Cordova, dead,
To life again, to hear thy buskin tread
And shake a stage; or when thy socks were on,
Leave thee alone for the comparison
Of all that insolent Greece or haughty Rome
Sent forth, or since did from their ashes come.
Triumph, my Britain! thou hast one to show,
To whom all scenes of Europe homage owe,
He was not of an age, but for all time;
And all the Muses still were in their prime,
When, like Apollo, he came forth to warm
Our ears, or like a Mercury to charm.
Nature herself was proud of his designs,
And joy'd to wear the dressing of his lines;
Which were so richly spun, and woven so fit,
As since she will vouchsafe no other wit:
The merry Greek, tart Aristophanes,
Neat Terence, witty Plautus, now not please;
But antiquated and deserted lie,
As they were not of Nature's family.
Yet must I not give Nature all; thy art,
My gentle Shakespeare, must enjoy a part:
For though the poet's matter nature be,
His art doth give the fashion; and that he
Who casts to write a living line, must sweat,—
Such as thine are,—and strike the second heat
Upon the Muse's anvil; turn the same,
And himself with it, that he thinks to frame;
Or, for the laurel, he may gain a scorn,—
For a good poet's made, as well as born:
And such wert thou. Look how the father's face
Lives in his issue; even so the race
Of Shakespeare's mind and manners brightly shines
In his well-tornèd and true-filèd lines;
In each of which he seems to shake a lance,
As brandish'd at the eyes of ignorance.
Sweet Swan of Avon, what a sight it were
To see thee in our waters yet appear,
And make those flights upon the banks of Thames,
That so did take Eliza and our James!
But stay; I see thee in the hemisphere

Advanc'd, and made a constellation there:
Shine forth, thou star of poets, and with rage
Or influence chide or cheer the drooping stage;
Which, since thy flight from hence, hath mourn'd like night,
And despairs day, but for thy volume's light.

BEN: JONSON.

NOTE ON THE EARLY EDITIONS OF SHAKESPEARE.

FOLIOS.

The First Folio was published in 1623, "printed by Isaac Jaggard and Edward Blount." It contains thirty-six plays (Pericles not being included in the Folios until 1664), arranged as Comedies, Histories, and Tragedies. Shakespeare's fellow-actors, John Heminge and Henry Condell, dedicate the volume to the brothers William, Earl of Pembroke [William Herbert], and Philip, Earl of Montgomery. In their address to the readers they profess to give for the first time the true text, and it is implied that they printed from Shakespeare's manuscripts. As a fact, the text abounds with errors, and in many instances they evidently print from the Quartos. In some cases the Folio gives a better text than the corresponding Quarto. It is the sole original authority for seventeen plays. The First Folio was reprinted by Upcott in 1807, and with great accuracy by Lionel Booth (1862–64). It has been reproduced with the aid of photographic processes by Staunton, and in a reduced form (under the superintendence of Halliwell-Phillipps) by Chatto and Windus.

The Second Folio, 1632.—Lowndes's statement that a copy exists with the date 1631 has not been verified. The printer was Thomas Cotes, and the property was vested in five booksellers. It is a reprint from the First Folio, with some errors corrected, some faultily altered to other erroneous readings, and many new errors added.

The Third Folio, "printed for Philip Chetwinde." There are two issues, 1663 and 1664.

The copies dated 1664 add "seven plays never before printed in Folio," viz.: Pericles, Prince of Tyre: The London Prodigal; The

History of Thomas Lord Cromwell; Sir John Oldcastle, Lord Cobham; The Puritan Widow; A Yorkshire Tragedy; The Tragedy of Locrine. These plays seem to have been selected because either the name of Shakespeare or the initials W. S. appear on the title-pages of the Quartos.

The Fourth Folio, 1685, includes the seven plays added in 1664.

QUARTOS.

In the following table the Quarto editions of the Poems and Plays are arranged in the order of the dates at which the first edition of each appeared. An asterisk points out the particular Quarto from which the text in the First Folio is printed.

Venus and Adonis, 1593, 1594, 1596, 1599, 1600, 1602, 1602, 1617, 1620, 1627 (at Edinburgh), 1630 ? (title-page lost), 1636.

Lucrece, 1594, 1598, 1600, 1607, 1616, 1624, 1632 (?), 1655.

Romeo and Juliet, 1597 (pirated and imperfect), 1599, *1609 ? (without date), 1637.

King Richard II., 1597, 1598, 1608, *1615, 1634.

King Richard III., 1597, 1598, 1602, 1605, 1612, 1622, 1629, 1634.

King Henry IV. Part I., 1598, 1599, 1604, 1608, *1613, 1622, 1632, 1639.

Love's Labour's Lost, *1598 (with Shakespeare's name on title, for the first time on any play), 1631.

The Passionate Pilgrim, 1599, 1612 (called third edition on title-page, but only two extant).

King Henry V., 1600 (pirated and imperfect), 1602, 1608 (both reprinted from 1600).

King Henry IV. Part II., 1600.

Much Ado About Nothing, *1600.

A Midsummer's Night's Dream, 1600 (printed for Fisher), *1600 (printed by Roberts).

The Merchant of Venice, 1600 (printed by Roberts), *1600 (printed for Heyes), 1637, 1652.

Titus Andronicus (? possibly a lost quarto of 1594), 1600, *1611.

The Merry Wives of Windsor, 1602, 1619 (both an imperfect report of the early form of the play), 1630.

Hamlet, 1603 (imperfect report of play in first form), 1604, 1605, 1611, ? undated, 1637.

King Lear, 1608, 1608 (both by same publisher), 1655.
Sonnets, 1609.
Troilus and Cressida, 1609, 1609.
Pericles, 1609, 1609, 1611, 1619, 1630, 1635.
Othello, 1622, 1630.

The "First Part of the Contention betwixt the two famous Houses of York and Lancaster" was printed in 1594 and 1600; the "True Tragedy of Richard Duke of York" in 1595 and 1600; the "Whole Contention" (in two parts) in 1619.

THE END.